Your Money, Your Life

Your Money, Your Life

Principles of
Financial Success

Randy Todhunter

BookLocker

Published by Booklocker Inc., 12441 N. Main Street, #38, Trenton, GA 30752-9998

ISBN: 978-1-64719-940-1
LCCN: 2021924125

Cover design by Jennifer Stimson
Printed on acid-free paper

This book is dedicated to my mom and dad,
Bill and Katie Todhunter,
who provided the foundation for understanding
financial success principles.

Praise for *Your Money, Your Life*

"Randy Todhunter has packed a lot of great stuff into this concise, easy-to-read book. I am impressed by the whole-life approach as he blends overall points of personal success with a philosophy for financial health. Teaching as he writes, he gives those who are new to personal finance an introduction to important concepts and vocabulary, as well as a practical framework to begin their journey."

> — Zena Featherston Marshall • Executive Director, Community & Business Partnerships, Fort Smith Public Schools

"If you are someone who wishes their financial decisions were more successful, this book is for you. Not only does Randy Todhunter describe the principles necessary to improve your financial situation, he also describes what it takes to live a successful life."

> — Wesley (Wes) B. Kemp • President & CEO – ABF Freight System Inc (Retired), Executive in Residence (Currently Serving), Walton College of Business, University of Arkansas

"Someone said, 'Put your money where your mouth is.' I'll spare you the wordy review and just tell you that I'm buying 25 copies of *Your Money, Your Life* to share with my adult children, nieces and nephews, young friends, and students I have the privilege of mentoring at my church and in our local schools."

> — Tim Bailey • President, Candy Craze

"I enjoyed this book very much! Mr. Todhunter surely met his goal with this easy to read, down-to-earth, and informative book. His writing style is exactly like talking to a favorite uncle."

> — Melinda Briscoe • Retired high school business teacher

"As someone who works with teenage students every day, simple straightforward truths about skills to succeed in life are needed more than ever. *Your Money, Your Life* is packed with understandable and bite-sized advice that will encourage and equip rather than overwhelm or criticize. Randy has put together a resource that can help create a firm foundation for your financial journey and be kept as an easily searchable source to pull off the shelf when needing a tip in any one of the many principles it covers."

— Braxton Schulte • Student pastor of Central Christian Church

"This book's title—*Your Money, Your Life*—says subtly what its pages cover in illuminating detail: money and life are intricately intertwined. The principles offered are as much about being your best self as they are about attaining financial success. The author is like a wise and friendly coach, warmly and patiently offering sound advice and gentle guidance for all stages of one's financial life, from preparing to start a career to retirement. Full of encouragement and simple terminology, it is an easy book to read, even for a financial novice. I recommend this book if you are looking for greater understanding and control of your money ... and your life."

— Chris Burton • Retired analytics executive for a large supply chain provider

"In this book, author Randy Todhunter not only hits on all cylinders for financial success, but his principles touch on many aspects for successful living! If you are struggling financially and need tools for finding your path to financial freedom, or if you just need encouragement to live your life with purpose, integrity, and a vision, this is the book for you! Well-written, in verbiage that meets even the most novice of readers looking for financial resources. A must read!"

— Jennifer Steele • EdS, Assistant Director of Athletics and Activities, Fort Smith Public Schools, Fort Smith, Arkansas

"Phenomenal! This book has the potential to change the course of many lives. There are so many good pointers that I will be revisiting it for many years to come!"

— Abigail Bramlett • College student

"Randy has written the perfect primer and reminder of the elements of sustainable success. He demonstrates that success is a function of planning, character, and skill, offering ways to grow in each. I love the tone of the book, as you can hear Randy cheering the reader along on every page."

— Kirby Clark • Vice President, Strategic Financial Planning & Analysis, ABF Freight

"My experience working with young adults has made it quite evident to me that obtaining financial success is neither something that is taught in schools nor something that can be done entirely with common sense. We need people like Randy, who drew on his vast experience of how to live a good financial life when writing in *Your Money, Your Life*. These helpful twenty-five fundamental principles about life and money are essential for young adults. That isn't frightening in this book; it's achievable. A young person who reads this book and applies its principles will be setting themselves up for success in life."

— Blake Pesetsky • Campus Pastor, Central Christian Church

"I didn't know a book could strike you with the sheer force of an 18-wheeler. *Your Money, Your Life* has crystal clear messages that rekindled a path for me to financial success. My spending was blinded by current trends and savvy marketing, but this book has allowed me to better understand my daily and life expenses. Young readers, it's time to be reminded that our finances are controlled by our own actions."

— Edward Merida • Social Media Coordinator/Corporate Recruiter, TEC Staffing Services

"Randy's new book is packed with seasoned wisdom. Every chapter challenges us to learn and grow to be better stewards of what God has blessed us with."

— Dr. Scott Clark • Chiropractor

"This book is encouraging, thought-provoking, and uplifting. A book that all high school students, especially juniors and seniors, as well as college students, would benefit from reading. I definitely enjoyed reading the book and would recommend it to others. It was exceptionally well-written in a way that made it an easy read, and explained finances in an easy-to-understand fashion.

"Randy also encourages the reader to take responsibility and change the course of their destiny, rather than placing blame on others for their failures. The reader is encouraged to believe in themselves regardless of past failures."

— Jan Marshall • Retired high school business teacher

"I found a lot of the principles very insightful and even wish I had heard some of the topics in your book while I was still in high school. I felt like your book was very well-written, and the conversational tone with the reader made it very easy for me to stay engaged. It was almost like you were actually talking to me.

"This book highlights several financial skills and concepts that many young adults are not exposed to during high school. Several chapters of the book not only highlight important financial skills but also important life skills."

— Sarah Emmons • Student at the University of Tulsa

"I found *Your Money, Your Life* to be a timely reminder of the principles of financial management without complex technical how-tos that may turn off a reader who thinks finances involves too much math. Todhunter's book passes down wisdom in identifying the guiding principles to everything financial in easily grasped concepts. The style is very readable and chapters can be read independently based on your needs. This is not a get-rich-quick book like so many but an investment (or reminder for some) in solid financial and life principles."

— Jeff Adams • Assistant Director, Career Services,
  for a public university

"If you are looking for a practical but detailed book on how to improve your financial situation, then *Your Money, Your Life* is for you. In his book Randy Todhunter shares principles on how you can become financially successful. He specifically mentions that if a person will treat the principles he shares with thoughtfulness and consideration, there will be a reward financially. The principles Randy shares will do that, but let me share that this book will require some thought and effort on your part. This is a very well-written and useful book. If your financial situation is broken or in need of repair, following the principles and guidance he gives will, without question, improve your finances."

— Bill Fink • Pastor and board member of Community Rescue
  Mission

"I believe young adults and above will benefit from this book. Young adults need to learn good habits/principles to live by and why it's important to be financially sound. But, as a 50-year-old, I also felt refreshed reading it, because Randy helped remind me of some principles I should live by.

"I feel like it was a great look into the psychology and mindset of a human as far as financial habits go. While reading, I felt more like I was receiving advice from a long-time friend/mentor.

"Randy's book is easy to read and follow. The chapters were short and sweet and held my attention. The writing style in the book has more of a communication with a friend feel to it."

— Jennifer Craig • High school business teacher

Contents

Introduction

"*Freethinkers are those who are willing to use their minds without prejudice and without fearing to understand things that clash with their own customs, privileges, or beliefs. This state of mind is not common, but it is essential for right thinking.*"

—Leo Tolstoy

This book is written for anyone who wishes they could do a better job of managing their money. You may be a high school or college student looking for some general financial advice and direction. Perhaps you've worked hard and tried to get out of debt and save, but it just hasn't seemed to work out. Maybe you want to invest a little, but you struggle to understand investing, finding it difficult to wrap your brain around investing concepts. Perhaps you want to change careers in order to increase your income, but you aren't sure if a change would help. You may also want to earn more money in order to be better prepared for retirement. In all of these cases, a deeper understanding of financial principles, and how to apply them in your life, can be most helpful.

Personal financial management is a broad subject about which much has been written. Sometimes, though, too much information can be overwhelming and perhaps confusing. I have attempted in this book to distill financial management down to some key principles that are of particular importance. As is often the case, mastery over a few crucial subjects can produce results as good as, or perhaps even better than, a smaller amount of knowledge about a broad range of topics. What I aim to do in this book is to help you, the reader, better understand the basic overall principles involved in personal money management.

My goal is to give you some tools so you can begin afresh managing your financial life in a way that slowly gets you out of debt, teaches you to shop and buy wisely, helps you save for retirement, and empowers you with the self-confidence that comes from being in control of your finances, rather than your finances being in control of you.

My aim is also to present these principles in easy-to-understand terms, since most of the concepts are simple in nature. The goal is not to teach you advanced techniques of finance and investing, but rather how to better manage your day-to-day life with regard to finances. It also includes a look at several aspects of life that may not seem to be directly related to financial management. Bear with me. I hope that, by the end of the book, you will agree that a key part of successful personal financial management is successful life management.

The format is informal in nature, and I invite you to read it as though you and I were able to sit down and chat about each chapter, perhaps at lunch each day. In ten to fifteen minutes, we could discuss and reflect on one chapter at a time.

Some chapters may offer you nothing new. Perhaps you have already mastered a specific topic and need only skim over the main points. Other chapters may speak directly to you and to your struggle for success. Take what is useful and helpful and what touches upon your need—or perhaps your heart.

You may feel that you already know as much as you need to know about personal finances, but I suspect, since you are reading the introduction, that you're seeking some new insights. Given how much this topic has been covered, my challenge is for you to be *open* as you read this book. *Open* to learning something new. *Open* to looking truthfully at the person you have become or are becoming. *Open* to making a change in your behavior. If you're not open to change and *willing* to change, then reading this book is pointless. It may give you some information, but if you don't *apply* that information to your life, then why waste your time reading it? You would be better served by doing something else that you are really interested in, and maybe even passionate about.

But . . . if you are ready to be open-minded about learning how to improve your finances, and how to better manage them and yourself, then I warmly invite you to join me in this exploration of financial success principles.

Financial Success Principles

L et's begin in this section by exploring the basic premise of this book: there are key *principles* involved in financial success. We will also consider the meaning of success— particularly success in the realm of finances. Finally, we'll assess if this book can be useful to you, and whether you can look forward to the prospect of success.

Let's get started.

Chapter 1

Is There a Need?

*"Too many people spend money they haven't earned, to buy
things they don't want, to impress people
that they don't like."*

—Will Rogers

I assume that you're asking yourself if this book can really help you. One way to answer that question is to invite you to assess how you're currently doing in your personal financial life. If you're pleased with the amount of your debt, your savings, your buying skills, and your investment plan for retirement, then I would like to congratulate you. You're doing well! If that's the case, then you probably don't need to read this book. You are already succeeding.

It might be useful, though, to consider with me for a minute the current state of household finances in the USA. Let's then examine whether that reveals a trend of overall success. Next, I invite you to compare your situation with what we find. It may be that your definition of success could use some tweaking. Perhaps this book might be helpful to you after all.

Credit Card Debt

Let's begin with debt—specifically, credit card debt. In the USA in 2021, the average household had $6,270 in credit card debt. Overall, Americans owed $807 billion across almost 506 million card accounts. Also, 45.4 percent of families carry some sort of credit card debt.[1]

Credit card debt has almost become synonymous with current-day life in America. A young high school or college student feels like they have finally "arrived" when they have their own credit card. Merchants promote their own brand of credit card, and it's become the de facto standard way to pay for most merchandise, whether purchased online or in a "brick and mortar" store. The use of such a card does offer convenience, without a doubt. In and of itself, having a credit card is not a problem; it can be a benefit. The issue comes when you don't pay off your balance in full each month. The interest rates that card companies charge are significantly higher than what you might pay for other consumer loans. As a result, many people struggle to get out from under the burden of monthly principal payments and associated steep interest payments. Consequently, the beauty of using a credit card has been soured by the monthly sucking sound of their hard-earned money draining away to the credit card companies.

What about you? Do you have credit card debt? If so, do you pay off the balance in full each month? If you do, you're using your credit card most effectively. If you do not, what interest rates are you paying on your various cards? I would wager that the average is well over 12 percent. If you've been late on any payments or missed payments, then you are now paying the dreaded "penalty rate," which can go as high as 29 percent or higher, depending on the card company. I think you would agree this is not the best use of your money.

Student Loan Debt

According to Nitro College, a company that evaluates how students and families can best pay for college (or pay off college debt), "Americans now owe more than $1.75 trillion in student loan debt, based on the most current figures available to Nitro. That money is not only owed by young people fresh out of college, but also by borrowers who have been out of school for a decade or more. The standard repayment timetable for federal loans is 10 years, but research suggests it actually takes four-year degree holders an average of 19.7 years to pay off their loans."[2]

Nitro also reported the following:

- One in four Americans have student loan debt—an estimated 44.7 million people
- Average student loan debt amount = $37,172
- Average student loan payment = $393/month[3]

Like credit card debt, student loan debt can be used judiciously to pay for attending college, earning a degree, and enabling a higher income over the span of one's career. Student loan debt often balloons far beyond what was envisioned when a person began their college experience though. Many factors should be considered when weighing the value of a college degree. Perhaps one of the most overlooked factors is the expected income of the selected career field. Many liberal arts degrees, for example, may help a person become better educated and well-rounded as a citizen, but they don't necessarily provide a pathway to a good financial future. With a lower-paying job, it can take decades to pay off an expensive student loan.

Do you have student loan debt? How much? How long will it take you to pay it off? If you have succeeded in keeping that type of debt at a modest level, then you're probably using it wisely to enable you to get a better-paying job. If you now find yourself saddled with a higher loan balance than you expected, you may be rethinking the wisdom of taking on so much debt and welcome any suggestions on how to best proceed with paying it down.

Savings

How are we doing as a nation regarding savings?

"Relatively small, unexpected expenses, such as a car repair or replacing a broken appliance, can be a hardship for many families without adequate savings. When faced with a hypothetical expense of $400, 61 percent of adults in 2018 say they would cover it, using cash, savings, or a credit card paid off at the next statement . . . Among the remaining 4 in 10 adults who would have more difficulty covering such an expense, the most common approaches include carrying a balance on credit cards and borrowing from friends or family . . . Twelve percent of adults would be unable to pay the expense by any means."[4]

What does your savings account balance look like? Are you living paycheck to paycheck, or are you confident that you could handle any short-term financial emergency? Do you have enough saved that you could handle a $400 emergency? How about a $1000 emergency? Do you regularly add to your savings account so that it is steadily growing?

Other Areas

What about your shopping skills? Do you feel that you make wise purchases, for the most part, or do your emotions get the best of you?

What about retirement? Have you started saving for retirement? Are you steadily adding to your retirement savings? Have you determined how much you need to save for retirement, and are you on track to accomplish that goal?

Are you happy with the money that you have invested? Do you feel your investments are successfully working for you? Where do you have your money invested, and what return are you getting?

Are you able to help others financially whenever you wish, or are you constrained by your financial situation and unable to do so?

Maybe you are one of those who has succeeded in getting a position that pays well. You might even have a six-figure income. Let's look at the surprising results of a 2021 survey among this group of individuals.

"High-earning millennials feel broke. Sixty percent of millennials raking in over $100,000 a year said they're living paycheck to paycheck, found a new survey by PYMNTS and LendingClub, which analyzed economic data and census-balanced surveys of over 28,000 Americans."[5]

If you're one of those high-earning individuals living paycheck to paycheck despite your income, does that feel like success to you? If not, then perhaps you, too, would be interested in some suggestions regarding financial principles.

Finally, are you both pleased and satisfied with your current level of financial success? What is your stress level, and how much of your stress is due to your finances? Life does not consist solely of your financial situation, and there are obviously many other aspects of life that bring enjoyment and satisfaction. But almost every area of your life can be impacted by your financial status. If you're experiencing stress due to your finances, then that stress will inevitably bleed over into every other area of your life, like dye seeping into a white towel.

If you now believe you could benefit from some new information and insights regarding personal financial success, then I encourage you to read on.

Chapter 2

What Is Success?

"That some achieve great success,
is proof to all that others can achieve it as well."

—Abraham Lincoln

L et's first talk about success in broad terms. Success in life is a common, almost universal, goal. Who doesn't want to be successful? But what is success, after all? There are perhaps as many answers to this question as there are people who might answer it. Surely some universal desires will emerge though. Good health, a loving family, a job that you enjoy and pays well, a circle of supportive friends, and opportunities to travel and enjoy leisure activities are often viewed as part of an overall successful life.

I would suggest that an important underpinning to all of these is the element of financial success. In order to have good health, you must be able to afford health insurance, nutritious food, medicine, and medical care. In order to cultivate a loving family life, one must successfully manage stress, and a common stressor for many is having financial problems. In order to promote a comfortable lifestyle, you must be able to afford decent housing, a reliable vehicle, and the occasional vacation. Many aspects of *overall success* require at least a basic amount of *financial success.*

It's certainly important to acknowledge that financial success does not necessarily result in overall success in life. A person can be very wealthy yet be unhappy. But without at least a basic amount of financial success, all the other components of success become much more difficult to achieve.

Some may wonder how much money it takes to consider yourself successful? Perhaps that's the wrong question. Let's examine the various things that go into becoming a financial success.

First of all, success can generally be defined as making excellent use of the resources you have at your disposal. Each of us has varied and diverse resources—time, health, energy, education, drive, passion, abilities, skills, a bank account, a job, and relationships with family and friends. These are all forms of assets that we "own." Success is being a good *steward*, or manager, of all that you have been entrusted with and making the best use of all of those resources. That is, in essence, the thrust of this book—to help you, the reader, learn how to maximize the effective use of all of your abilities and assets, especially the financial ones.

Although financial success can certainly mean something different to each person, let's define it for the purposes of this book. Financial success would include having enough resources to maintain a comfortable standard of living, being able to handle short-term financial emergencies, being able to sufficiently save for retirement, and being able to help others financially.

Note that financial success does not mean "getting rich." This book is not about how to get rich. As we now know, having a certain *amount* of money does not guarantee that one feels "rich" anyway. Another way to put it is to pose the question, "How much money is enough?" Invariably, the answer that most people give is, "Just a little more!" That answer seems to hold true whether the person has a net worth of $10,000, $100,000, or $1,000,000! Whether you consider yourself rich or not is thus more of a mindset than a particular dollar amount of assets accumulated. *(See Chapter 9 for a discussion of the definition and importance of net worth.)*

If success were simply based on the size of your bank account, then the only truly successful people would be the richest people in the world, those worth several hundred billion dollars each. But logic tells us that there are far more people who enjoy financial success than just a small handful of ultra-wealthy individuals.

It also depends upon with whom you compare yourself. A pastor friend of mine once went on a mission trip to Africa. While there, he talked with a local who asked him if he was rich back in America. The pastor replied that he was definitely *not* rich. In response, the local asked him a few questions.

"Do you have a home?"

"Do you have running water?"

"Do you have an inside toilet?"

"Do you have a car, or more than one?"

"Do you have a bank account?"

One by one, the pastor had to answer that, yes, he had all of these. In the mind of the local, and in the context of *his* culture, the pastor was clearly rich! We tend to compare ourselves to those who seem to be doing better than us. Perhaps a better approach would be to compare ourselves with the rest of the world, which includes many countries where even basic services such as clean water and good medical care may not be widely available.

In order to experience true contentment, it's important to understand how each of us defines and views success. Can a tradesman living in a modest house think of himself as successful? Yes! It does not require a certain level of income, size of house, or any other specific criteria to be a success. It simply means that you're making wise use of the resources that you have, whatever they may be.

Can we be successful while still striving to improve and better ourselves? If we feel successful, does that mean we don't need to try anymore? If we have some measure of success, should we simply maintain that level or push forward to achieve more financially? In other words, is success a destination that you arrive at, or is it more of a process? Let's look deeper into these questions.

There is an interesting dichotomy that each of us must embrace: 1) We should continually strive to improve and be the best we can be. 2) We need to be content with what we have. In that context, contentment—or success—does not mean that the person doesn't try anymore or doesn't see the need to work hard to improve and become better. But he is able to appreciate and enjoy where he is in life, financially, right now. Being content, yet always seeking to grow and do better, is the goal. If we don't embrace both contentment and ambition, we run the risk of swinging to one extreme or the other. We may feel completely satisfied with whatever measure of success we have experienced and believe we don't need to learn anything more or strive to grow. In effect we stagnate at our current level of success. Or, on the other hand, we may become obsessed with always getting more and more, consumed by this need to always be better and richer, robbing ourselves of any sense of contentment in the present.

It's also important to note that the definition of success varies depending upon one's stage in life. *(See Appendix 5 for a description of The Stages of Life.)* A common pitfall for some is the expectation that in order to be successful they should have the same standard of living as those who are middle-aged or older, perhaps even retired. This expectation fails to consider that others have had decades to steadily accumulate their wealth. Is a high school student not a success because they haven't yet graduated from college? Is a college student not a success because they don't yet have a job? Is a new employee, early in their career, not a success because they haven't yet accumulated any assets? No. These people can all be considered successful right where they are, even though their financial assets may be meager. In this same way you can be successful at every stage of your life, even though your standard of living and savings may vary dramatically from one stage to the next.

Success can be realized and enjoyed all along life's journey. If you don't recognize and embrace this truth, then success can become an elusive prize that will always be just out of reach. In that case, sadly, a person may live their entire life never really feeling like a success. But if they would just step back and assess what they have accomplished, they could see the many small successes they've experienced throughout their life. Two people can live almost exactly the same life—same job, city, marital status, income—yet their attitude will determine their feelings of success. One will be filled with delight; the other will be filled with despair. The glass is either half full or half empty, but it's still the same glass. The only difference is in what you focus on.

Now that we have considered what constitutes success in life, both personally and financially, let's look at the principles at work as we interact with money in our lives.

Chapter 3

Principles of Financial Success

"Nature does not ask your permission, she has nothing to do with your wishes, and whether you like her laws or dislike them, you are bound to accept her as she is, and consequently all her conclusions."

—Fyodor Dostoyevsky

We are all familiar with the various laws of nature. For example, if you hold out an object and let it drop, it will fall to the ground. This illustrates the law of gravity. Another aspect of nature's laws is described by Bernoulli's Principle and Newton's laws of motion. They explain what enables an airplane to fly, or a sailboat to skim across the water at right angles to the direction of the wind. These are all examples of the physical principles, or laws, that characterize our world.

I would suggest that just as there are physical principles, or laws, at work in our physical world, there are also principles at work in our financial world. These are similar to the physical principles in many ways, such as being predictable and repeatable. Many of these are based on simple math, such as how compound interest works. Others are more connected to human nature, such as the psychological impact that becoming debt-free has on a person.

Principles are also like the laws of nature in that we don't create them; instead, we discover them. We can choose to believe them or not, but that doesn't change whether or not they are true. If we choose to believe that gravity will not apply at our house, then we may decide to jump off the roof and soar to the house across the street. In spite of our disbelief in gravity, the law will nonetheless apply, and our "flight" to the neighbor's house will be very short-lived indeed!

In the same way, if we choose to ignore the principles of financial success, we will find ourselves dealing with disappointment and our dreams will be unrealized. The more you deviate from these principles, the more you will struggle, just as an airplane's wing will not perform as well if it deviates from its optimal shape.

I have compiled twenty-five essential principles of financial success that I want to share with you. I'm sure there are many more that could have been included here, some of which you might feel are even more important. You also might not agree that all of these are true principles. I just ask that you have an open mind and consider that these just *may* be true. If so, wouldn't it be good to know about and heed them?

In order to utilize the principles of financial success, you must do several things.

First of all, you must not only learn them; you must be open to the fact that they are true. If you don't accept and believe that these principles are observable facts, then you have cut away the motivation to persevere, to hang in there when implementing the principles becomes tough. Thus, the first step is to understand, acknowledge, and accept the truth of the principles.

The second step, which is perhaps the most difficult of all, is to summon the self-discipline to live in accordance with the principles. It's one thing to acknowledge a truth. It's quite a different matter to change yourself to live in harmony with that truth. Learning is important, but application is the secret of success, not knowledge. Even when you're succeeding, there will always be periodic setbacks and challenges that no one else may see or know about. But you will know about them, and they will tempt you to slow down, back off, and give up. That's when patience and diligence must step to the front and keep you in the game.

You must then embrace the third step, which is to continually learn new truths about financial principles as you move through life. This lifelong learning process can be illustrated by viewing it as though encountering a series of walls.

Navigating hurdles to growth

Let each wall represent a point in life where you're not sure how to proceed, financially speaking. You don't know what to do to get past the immediate hurdle you are facing. Each hurdle can be thought of as a wall with a door in it. There is a key that hangs next to the door, which can be used to open it. The key represents a financial principle, or truth, that you need to learn, understand, and apply at that point in your life. Taking the key and unlocking the door lets you go through and move on to the next wall, or phase, in your life.

But if you choose not to learn that there is a key available (if you are not open to that truth), then you will remain stuck at that wall. You can search the surface of the wall for an opening, run into it with all your might, plead with it, curse it, and beat on it, but you will not get past it.

The same will happen if you let yourself be open to the truth, learn about the key, but then choose to *not* reach out and grasp it. For whatever reason, you may think that either you don't need the key, or you simply don't want to use it. Maybe you feel that it's your lot in life to remain stuck behind this particular wall.

Whatever your reasons are for choosing to not use the key, the results will be the same. You will not get past the wall, which represents the hurdle that's before you at this point in your life. It will remain as a barrier to your progress.

That is life, is it not? Continually learning new truths, assessing how we should respond to those truths, then changing or adapting so that our lives will be in concert with, and in harmony with, those truths.

Growing Requires Perseverance

As a final observation, note that we all have the option to stop this growth process, to decide that we are tired and don't want to learn anymore. We don't want to continue to assess and evaluate new truths, or do the hard work of adapting to them. That's the tug and pull that we all have to work against all our lives. The lure of the ease of mediocrity. Just relax. Coast. Shift into neutral. This learning, thinking, and changing is hard work and tiresome. Therefore the siren call of comfort is continually whispering to us that we don't need to be doing all this. "Take it easy. You deserve it." This call is almost explicit in saying, "Don't think about retirement. Don't think about ten years from now. Just think about *today!* Think about what you need or want or *deserve* to have today!" Of course, if you "deserve" it today, then you must do whatever it takes to make that happen, right? Which often involves a credit card or other form of consumer debt. After all, you deserve it, and you deserve it *right now!* And so it goes . . .

As you read and mull over the principles that we will examine in the following chapters, I encourage you to keep an open mind to the validity of each of them. See if you don't come to agree with me that these are, indeed, principles that will reward you with success if you learn and apply them to your life.

Chapter 4

Can *You* Succeed?

"If you think you can or you can't, you're right."

—Henry Ford

Managing your personal finances is really more about human nature than about mathematical and accounting principles. If we understand, account for, and manage the tendencies of our human nature, we will be successful. If we do not, success will be elusive, no matter how well we understand the world of finance. It's as though we have two opposing forces within us. One is working for our long-term good; one is working for our short-term pleasure. If we don't consciously and diligently pay heed to, and follow, the force working toward our long-term good, then the short-term pleasure impulses will win out every time.

You may have tried many things thus far in your life as part of your effort to be financially successful. There could be many reasons why your success has been less than you would like for it to be. We will explore some of these together in the following chapters. But the upshot may be that you now feel the cards are stacked against you. You feel unable to succeed no matter what you do. You're no longer *expecting* to succeed! As a result, your own expectations are working against you.

Books have been written on the integral relationship between our expectations and the results that we experience. Jack Canfield has written an inspiring book on this topic titled *The Success Principles*. The key takeaway from his book, and others like it, is that our personal expectations have a powerful influence on our lives and on our success. These authors assert that each of us has far more capacity for success than we may realize. I encourage you to read his book, but for now I invite you to simply be aware of these two observations: 1) you *can* be a success, and 2) your own expectations largely determine your ability to succeed.

You may protest that you don't have a degree in finance, or perhaps you may not have a college degree at all. Maybe you were not born into wealth, don't feel that you have superior intelligence, and lack special abilities to set you apart, and thus ahead. Therefore, in your mind, you believe you don't have what it takes to succeed. Your negative self-belief stings, but you try to be realistic, possibly resigning yourself to what you feel is a locked and negative reality.

I would challenge your assumptions, though, with the reminder that people from all walks of life, with or without college degrees, born into wealth or not, and without any particular abilities have been successful. Andrew Carnegie is one such example.

Carnegie was born into a poor family in Dunfermline, Scotland, where his father worked as a handloom weaver and his mother sold potted meats. They emigrated to the United States in 1848, when Carnegie was only twelve, and he began working as a bobbin boy in a cotton mill. At that young age, he changed bobbins for twelve hours a day, six days a week. From those humble beginnings, through hard work and determination, he eventually became one of the wealthiest men in America. He is further noted to be one of the greatest philanthropists ever, donating the equivalent of over $77 billion in today's dollars. He funded many worthwhile projects in his lifetime, including financial backing for over three thousand libraries. In spite of his background he became an outstanding success.

Perhaps you feel that you've made too many mistakes and bad choices throughout your life and therefore cannot overcome the consequences of those decisions. Before you throw in the towel and resign yourself to a lifetime without success, let me share another perspective. I have probably made many of the same mistakes that you have made. In fact, that's the way I've learned much of what I share in this book—by making poor choices and then trying to learn from them. Recognize and become comfortable with the fact that you, too, will experience failures along the way. But a single failure does not make a failed life. We all fail from time to time. The only way *not* to fail is to never try anything.

Prepare yourself for that day of failing by envisioning it happening, and then decide in advance how you will respond to it. Determine that you will not get rattled, but instead, step back and assess where you went astray in your plans, or the execution of those plans, then decide what you will do differently. See yourself as being self-confident, capable, and unruffled by any setbacks. Speak this reminder: "I expected that to happen occasionally." Then, put it behind you and move on. The key thing is to recognize and accept that you *will* have some failures and setbacks along the way. That is a normal, natural aspect of growth. A baby doesn't learn to walk without falling down a few times, perhaps even in a painful way. She doesn't give up trying to walk though. She gets back up and tries it, again and again. And so will you.

Good financial management doesn't have to be heavy, hard, and oppressive. It can be rather fun and liberating. But it does require self-discipline. Just as raising children means you have to sometimes discipline them; you will need to practice self-discipline. The disciplining of children results in them growing into competent and wise adults. Your disciplining of yourself results in you doing what is best for your life, thus enabling you to succeed.

Finally, recognize that when you are young, your most important income-generating asset is you—your energy, passion, creativity, and strength. You can utilize all of these abilities in your job, and they can significantly impact your income. When you first begin your working life, *you* may be the only asset you have to offer, but don't discount the value and impact of that. The goal is to leverage this asset—yourself—using it to its greatest advantage.

You may very well require some additional training, education, and practice to attain success. That's part of the process for everyone. If you determine that you *will* succeed, though, then you now have unlocked the capability for that to happen.

What is the key to success? Persistence and perseverance, combined with a calm, confident certainty that you *will* prevail, that you *will* succeed.

Principles About Life

W e now begin our look in detail at each of the principles presented in the book. The first ones to be examined are not focused directly on finances. Rather, they are more general in nature but critically important to every area of life, including managing your finances. If you don't understand and live in harmony with these general life principles, then your efforts at developing financial skills will be severely hobbled. It will be like running a race with heavy ankle weights. It's only when you grasp the meaning of these life principles and determine to live in accordance with them that those weights will drop away.

Chapter 5

Principle of Actions Have Consequences

"There are in nature neither rewards nor punishments—there are consequences."

—Robert G. Ingersoll

PRINCIPLE 1:
Actions Have Consequences.

W e are all familiar with the idea that our actions have consequences. If we take a walk and get caught in a downpour without an umbrella, then we get wet. If we put our hand on a hot stove, then we get burned. If we cross a room in the dark, we may stub our toe. You get the idea. The challenge is in trying to accept the fact that this is true in virtually every area of life. You might even call it the "if/then" principle. *If* you do this, *then* that will happen. It gets much harder to see this in more complex areas of life, but it's true nonetheless. For example, *if* you fail to save for retirement throughout your adult working life, *then* you will not have a retirement nest egg when you retire. *If* you allow your temper to flare up frequently, *then* you will damage your relationships with others. *If* you focus on negative thoughts, *then* you will be an unhappy person. *If* you choose to not maintain your vehicle, *then* it will wear out much more quickly (and may strand you on the side of the road!).

What we sometimes fail to consider is that *inaction* has consequences as well as action. For example, you have the opportunity to *choose* the life you wish to experience, but you can also *not* make that choice and opt to just let happen what will happen. In this case, you are, by default, choosing not to act. Let's consider an illustration from nature to better understand the consequences of inaction compared to action.

If you don't choose the direction of your life, then you're like a twig floating down a river—the river of life, in this case. You go where the current takes you. Sometimes you may get caught up in brush on the shore and be stuck there for a few hours, days, or even years. You may end up in a backwater area that's calm and still, but the water there isn't as fresh. You may pass by some very interesting things on the shore, but you can't stop to look at them.

On the other hand, if you are like a small otter rather than a twig, then you can choose where you go in the river of life. You can swim across to the other shore, downstream with the current at a rapid pace, or even swim upstream. If you're strong enough, you can make headway against the current. The point is that the otter is *choosing* where he wishes to go. He may make some poor choices, but they will be his choices. He will learn from those poor choices and gradually get better at being a successful roamer of the river.

You get to similarly choose how you live your life, if you act and decide to do so. This not only applies to your career choice, but to your choices on whom you marry, where you live, and in the way that you manage your finances. This is a liberating opportunity, but only if you recognize it, own it, and embrace it. You can be like the otter and actively choose what you do with your life, or you can be like the twig floating downstream and let circumstances and others make your life choices for you.

If you choose to improve your financial life, it will probably mean that you'll need to assess what financial education you need, both now and ongoing. Education is often viewed as something that you get primarily while attending school as a child or young adult. It is true that we learn much during those years, but as adults, we are also responsible for our own ongoing education. We *choose* to learn more about cooking, car maintenance, woodworking, gardening, or whatever interests us. Learning more about financial management is one more aspect of lifetime learning.

If you pursue additional education regarding financial management, *then* you will acquire skills and equip yourself for new opportunities. You will grow. If you neglect to consistently educate yourself and stay updated in this field, then you will remain at your present level of knowledge and skill. That will limit your earning potential and thus impact your financial goals. You have the capacity to learn so much more, but for that to happen you have to choose to devote the time and energy it requires.

Achieving success also requires that you take good care of yourself. *If* you choose to eat nutritious foods, get regular exercise, sleep seven to eight hours a night, and manage your stress, *then* you will operate at your peak capacity. To the degree that you ignore your physical and mental health, your ability to be successful will be diminished. This is another example of our actions having consequences.

Everything we do, including what we think and say, does have consequences. Success in managing our finances is directly dependent upon what we do. If we study financial management and apply ourselves to doing what is recommended, we will make progress. If we don't apply ourselves to learning and then acting on what we learn, our situation will remain unchanged.

Chapter 6

Principle of Personal Accountability

"You must take personal responsibility.
You cannot change the circumstances, the seasons,
or the wind, but you can change yourself.
That is something you have charge of."

—Jim Rohn

PRINCIPLE 2:
You Are Responsible for Your Life.

I n many areas of our lives, we receive direction from others. If we work for someone else, we probably have a supervisor who gives us assignments and provides directions on how the job must be done. This direction can be very detailed, such as instructions to a new employee on their first day. It can also be general and loosely defined, like when an experienced employee will be working on something with which they are very familiar. We also receive direction from various governmental offices. This encompasses everything from how your taxes must be prepared to the legal requirements for titling a car.

We are given a lot of direction as children, primarily from our parents and teachers. This guidance is intended to enable us to eventually direct our own lives—to become productive citizens and contributors to society. In many ways, it's much easier to have someone else telling us what to do and making complicated decisions for us. Then we don't have to spend the mental energy trying to figure out what action to take. But it's certainly the mark of being an adult to assume the mantle of "decision maker" of your own life. You choose what type of career you would like to have, where to live, whom to marry, and all of the other things that go into making a life.

In many ways, my goal in this book is to provide you with a basic understanding of the knowledge and skills involved in successfully managing your financial life. It's important, though, to weigh and recognize that in order for this to come about, there isn't anyone who will be giving you directions on how to accomplish your life goals. You have complete freedom as an adult to spend, save, borrow, and invest as much or as little as you like. That is a wonderful privilege, one which we largely enjoy because we live in a country that values individual freedom. But that also means that if you *don't* decide to manage yourself well—personally and financially—it won't automatically happen. Each of us is personally accountable for how well we do in life financially.

When we don't succeed at something, there is a natural tendency to think that it may be someone else's fault. And so, we protest with our excuses.

> "I didn't get the right kind of parenting when I was
> growing up."
> "I wasn't born into a wealthy family."
> "I didn't get the opportunity to go to the college or the
> trade school I wanted because my grades weren't good
> enough."
> "My grades were poor because my teachers didn't do a
> good job of teaching me."

If we have an outlook like these examples illustrate, then we shy away from the uncomfortable truth that almost everything that happens to us in life as an adult is because of decisions that *we* have made, whether good or bad, not decisions made by someone else.

You don't have to "settle" for the lot you've been dealt in life. But in order to be successful, you must make the decision that *you* are going to apply yourself—to educate yourself and develop new skills, thereby expanding your capacity and abilities.

If you have not had the success you desire, I challenge you to look in the mirror and recognize that you are very likely looking at the source of your problems. Other people, or external circumstances, don't run your life—you do! Each of us has a choice; we can either *run* our lives or *ruin* them. Note that the only difference between *run* and *ruin* is the letter *I*. It's when you let yourself become self-centered, when you let an emphasis on what *I* want, when *I* want it, distort and corrupt your effort to *run* your life, that things go downhill. You have to control that urge for short-term pleasure in order to successfully *run* your life.

What we all deserve is what we have, if we live in a free country, and that is *opportunity*! We don't deserve to be cared for by someone else. We don't deserve to be cared for by the government. We deserve the opportunity to think for ourselves. We deserve the opportunity to learn. And we deserve the opportunity to choose how we want to live our lives. Whatever we expect to receive, we should expect to have to earn it. There is no free lunch!

Success in managing our finances is up to us. That can be both liberating and terrifying. No one else is responsible for our lives or our happiness. We are. Nothing will change unless we change. Take charge of your life! Don't let any excuses get in the way of achieving your goals.

Chapter 7

Principle of Risk

"The biggest risk is not taking any risk."

—Mark Zuckerberg

PRINCIPLE 3:
Rewards Come from Managing Risk, Not Fearing It.

I f something is described as "being risky," that usually means it has the potential to turn out badly and should probably be avoided. Walking across a raging river on a wet, moss-covered log would certainly be considered risky by almost anyone. Darting across a six-lane freeway would also definitely be considered risky. But is risk always bad? Is it possible that there might be something useful about risk? Perhaps there might even be a place for risk in your financial planning.

Risk can generally be defined as an assessment of the likelihood that a bad outcome will occur. For example, you may be in a hurry and find yourself speeding as you drive to an important appointment. You may have considered what the *risk* would be that you could get stopped by the police and issued a speeding ticket. Your assessment would initially include two components.

The first is an assessment of how *likely* it is that you will get stopped. If you know there is often a policeman doing speed checks on your route, you may decide the likelihood is high that you will be pulled over.

The second is an assessment of how *bad* the consequences would be if you did get stopped. It's possible that you may just get a warning and nothing more. It's also possible that you could get an expensive ticket, have your insurance rates go up, and perhaps have to attend a defensive-driving class.

There is an important third component of risk, though, one which we often don't think about or consciously assess. That is the emotional component. In our example above, what we have not mentioned is how you might *feel* about getting stopped for speeding. Perhaps you take pride in being a law-abiding citizen and would be embarrassed if you were stopped, whether you were given a ticket or just a warning. In that case, your feelings about getting stopped might tip the scales in the direction of not speeding.

Let's say that your feelings are different than that though. You feel that laws are created to provide overall safety and security to our world. But you also feel that it isn't a big deal if you break a law occasionally, as long as no one gets hurt. In that case, your feelings about getting stopped would probably leave you inclined to speed, or at least your feelings surrounding it would not be a factor that would inhibit your speeding.

The point is that our feelings about a situation can have a powerful influence on our perception of risk. Those feelings can even override any logical assessment of the risk involved. Let's look at another example. Suppose you read an article about someone who ventured out over the guard rails at the Grand Canyon and tragically slipped and fell to their death.

You now have to assess what you've read and decide what you will do in response. Will you decide that going to the Grand Canyon is altogether too risky and determine never to even drive there? Will you decide to visit but stay back at least a hundred feet from the edge? Or will you decide that it's safe as long as you stay behind the guard rails and don't go within ten feet of the edge?

Most people would agree that deciding to *never* go to the Grand Canyon at all would be an overreaction to the perceived risk. In so doing, you would be depriving yourself of getting to see the beauty and majesty of one of America's truly great landmarks. You may snort and reply that no one would be so fearful that they would decide to never go to the Grand Canyon.

But isn't that what people do when they observe someone losing a lot of money in the stock market? They see another's loss, and in order to protect themselves, they decide that they will *never* go near it at all. They are fearful they might fall also—not to their death, but to their financial ruin.

Perhaps the reason they are afraid is because they don't know where the edge is. They don't know the falling-off point. So to be safe, they decide to stay completely away from the "edge" altogether.

As you learn more about finances and investing, my hope is that you will gain a better knowledge of where the edge is—where it starts to become risky, and even dangerous. As you acquire that knowledge, you may realize that there are many investments that still leave you a hundred feet back from the edge, or even farther. They allow you see most of the beauty before you, yet still remain safe.

Reckless vs. Calculated Risks

Let's look at another interesting aspect of risk. We all possess the ability to affect the level of risk in any situation. We can, therefore, change a *reckless* risk into a *calculated* risk.

The mountain climber makes his risk calculated rather than reckless by doing several things. First, he learns all that he can about the mountain, the route, and the weather. Next, he studies and practices techniques, then learns about the best equipment available and invests in it. He keeps himself strong by exercising and practicing using the same muscles that he will use on the climb. On the day he begins the climb, he will try to eat the best breakfast possible—one that will provide long-lasting energy. He tries to assess all of the problems or challenges that could arise, then determines how he would handle them. He tries to uncover whether there is any potential problem that could occur that he could not recover from. If he determines there is a potentially disastrous risk, he does not make the climb that day. There could be a potential for a severe thunderstorm in the forecast, for example. By deliberately taking all of these steps, he has taken what would be a reckless risk and changed it into a calculated risk. He is managing the risk that he is taking.

Risk in Buying a Car

Another, more common, example of risk management would be buying a used car. You have decided to purchase a previously owned vehicle and want to choose one that is not only attractive and appealing, but one that's reliable and offered at a fair price. In effect, you want to reduce the risk that you will buy a lemon, a problem car that will be a source of exasperation rather than joy. So how do you do that? How do you turn the purchase of a used car from a reckless risk into a calculated risk?

First of all, if you simply walk up to the first nice-looking car on the lot and offer to buy it without first checking out its mechanical condition and at least starting the engine, I think you would agree that would be considered a *reckless* risk. Since you don't know anything about the car other than what you can see at a glance, there's a significant possibility that something could be wrong with it. Because you elected not to learn more about it, you're allowing yourself to take a reckless risk.

On the other hand, let's assume that you begin to ask questions in order to learn more about the car before you decide whether or not to make an offer on it. You first visually examine the car, carefully looking for any observable defects. You're doing your best to ascertain the true condition of the car, asking questions as well as taking it for a test drive. You assess many things as you attempt to determine how *likely* it is that the car will have a problem and *how bad* the consequences will be if that problem occurs. You attempt to learn the following:

- What is the overall condition?
- What is the mileage?
- How well has it been cared for?
- How worn are the tires?
- What features does it have?
- How well does it handle, accelerate, and feel on the road?
- Does everything function properly, or is anything malfunctioning—however minor?
- What is the repair history of this year and model, based on consumer reporting?
- How much does it cost, and is that a fair market price?

By learning these details about the car, you have greatly reduced the risk that there will be something unexpected about it that you didn't discover. There is still a risk that there *could* be problems with it, but by doing your research, you now feel confident that the risk is low. You are now taking a *calculated* risk, not a reckless risk, that there may be any problems with the car.

Risk in Finances

We can approach our finances in much the same way, decreasing our risk by researching and learning about what we are considering. Let's say that you have decided you're ready to buy stock in a company. You've established a brokerage account, familiarized yourself with how to use their website, and have transferred funds into your new account. You are now ready to buy stock and have a particular stock in mind that you like. How do you decrease the risk that it will be a poor choice, a risky investment?

Just as you did with shopping for a used car, you learn as much as you can about the company. Again, you are trying to determine how *likely* it is that the investment will be a poor one, and *how bad* the consequences will be if that turns out to be the case. You will try to find out information about many aspects of the company.

- How long have they been in business?
- What products or services do they sell, and are they in demand?
- What competition do they have, and are they themselves a strong competitor?
- Are their profits growing? What about their revenue? Is it staying flat or falling?
- What has their stock price been doing over the past three months, year, and two years?
- What is the opinion of the investor community of this stock?

There is a chapter devoted to investing later in the book, but this example illustrates that you can decrease the risk of investing in a stock, or of taking any other financial action you may be considering. Just as you decreased the risk of buying a car that is a lemon by learning more about it, you can do the same thing with an investment you're contemplating. In both cases, you have changed your action from being a reckless risk to a calculated risk.

Calculated risks are an important part of advancing financially in many ways—buying a home, moving to a new city or to a new job, or even changing careers. These are all examples of calculated financial risks.

I say all of this because the potential financial payoff is much greater for those investments that *do* have a little risk associated with them. Investing in the stock market, for example, carries more risk than putting your money into a bank savings account. But your investment in the stock market has the potential to grow significantly more than a savings account. By learning more about investing, about the stock market, and about individual stocks, you can transform your investment decisions into calculated risks rather than reckless ones.

One final observation is that any change carries with it some risk. If you decide to make some changes in how you manage your financial life, there is a risk that it might not work out like you expect. There is a risk that your financial life may become worse. To the extent that you let your *feelings* about that risk determine your assessment of the risk involved, you increase the likelihood that your fear will overcome your logic, and you will not make any changes. I encourage you to let your increased knowledge about finances become your preferred tool for assessing risk, rather than your feelings. Change *is* risky. But change also opens your life up to new possibilities. Assess risk, weigh it, and decrease it by learning about what you are changing.

Risk is a part of life. We all take small risks every day. Some risks are insignificant and not worth worrying about. Other risks are bigger and warrant our careful consideration. Through study and observation, you can deliberately and confidently take calculated risks rather than reckless ones. In so doing, you are managing risk rather than letting risk, and your feelings about it, manage you.

Chapter 8

Principle of Habit

"We become what we repeatedly do."

—Sean Covey

PRINCIPLE 4:
Habits Are Either Your Servant or Your Master.

Habits are an interesting aspect of life. To enable us to be more efficient, human nature includes the ability to learn to do actions automatically, without thinking. This frees up our minds to think about other things. If we didn't have the ability to develop habits, we would have to consciously think about, and guide, every minute detail of every action we took throughout the day, no matter how many times we had done it previously. Consider how much time and energy it would require to do even small tasks, like buttoning your shirt or blouse. You would need to concentrate and focus just as though you had never done it before. Your whole day would be filled with small, repetitive actions like this.

Much of what we consider to be our personality is the sum total of the hundreds of habitual ways we act and react every day. Habits can even be seen in the way we respond to situations. If you see something you want to buy, what action do you typically take? Do you stop and consider how much you may have already spent this month, or do you whip out your credit card without thinking? What is your *habitual* response?

If someone says something to you that could be construed as hurtful, how do you respond? Do you pause and consider that they may not have meant it the way it sounded? Perhaps they are simply having a bad day. Or do you react quickly in anger, firing back with harsh words that you later regret? Your typical response is your habitual response, your *habit*.

Habits, good or bad, are powerful. Habits, by definition, oppose change. They work tirelessly without you even being aware of them so that you keep doing the same things. When you attempt to change an action that is habitual, that habit will steadily and persistently resist your efforts. Once a habit has become ingrained, it can be hard to break. Experts tell us that it takes approximately twenty-one to thirty days of deliberate effort to break an old habit or start a new one. It may take even longer for some people.

For this reason, good habits can be one of your greatest allies in setting a new course in your life. Once you get a new, good habit established, the power of that habit will keep you propelled in that new direction. You will have to consciously and deliberately work *against* this new habit in order to fall back into your old ways.

Bad habits have this same power, though, and can possibly be your greatest enemy as you are trying to change. If you only attempt a change for a week or two, then let yourself lapse back into the old habit, you will have let it immediately move back to a position of power and influence in your life. Worse yet, this lapse will discourage you. You will be tempted to think that you can never overcome this habit. You might feel as if it's pointless to even try. This is who you are, after all.

Habits can make it feel like it's impossible to change. Maybe you have tried to make a change and failed, time and time again. But I would like to suggest that you *can* change any single routine action, any habit, no matter what it might be, if you are motived to do so. Let me ask you to consider for a minute the following hypothetical situation. I realize this is somewhat gruesome, but hopefully it drives home the point about your true ability to implement change.

Let's suppose that you have a companion who will be by your side throughout your day today. His job is to watch carefully to see if you fall back into a specific old habit that you're trying to break. If you slip up and lapse back into your old habit, he will ask you to extend your hand and will then chop off one of your fingers! He will quickly provide a medical wrapping, along with appropriate medication so that it will heal successfully, but your finger will be gone—forever!

Now if that were really the situation today, do you think that you could manage to go all day and not succumb to that bad habit? I think you could. And if that companion is going to be with you the next day and the next, for a full thirty days, could you manage to control your actions for more than one day? Perhaps for the full thirty days? I believe you could, because you would be highly motivated!

The most important point of this chapter is that when you attempt to make a change, such as how you manage your financial life, you are changing your *habits*. So in order to be successful in making any change, you must recognize and use proven tactics for changing habits. Here are some suggested strategies to employ:

- Be convinced of the value of the change you're making. If you're not completely convinced that this change is both worthwhile and important, your resolve will be weak.
- Steel yourself to the truth that changing a habit is *hard!* Be prepared to diligently focus on it every day.
- Resolve that you *can* deliberately create a new habit— recall the story about losing a finger.

- Try to change only one habit at a time. Remember that each habit has power that will require energy and focus in order to turn it around. If you try to change too many at once, they will overcome your reservoir of resolve and drag you right back into all your old habits.
- Be dogged about sticking with the new habit, every day, for a full thirty days.
- Remember that your goal is to make the habit your servant. Refuse to let it be your master.

The ability to overcome a habit requires you to *understand* how habits work, then to *take action* in order to break a habit or form a new one. Habits cannot be ignored. You must learn and adopt the strategies needed to create new habits and overcome old ones; otherwise, you will be fighting an unseen enemy each day, who will seemingly resist you at every turn.

Principles About the Psychology of Money

L et's now explore the principles of wealth and how we define it, including the important impact of debt and net worth upon our psyche, which is often overlooked. In this section, we will also examine the psychological impact of money. We conclude with the principle about "knowing thyself" and do an assessment of the importance of looking within—of examining your personal assumptions, beliefs, and weaknesses regarding money.

Chapter 9

Principle of Net Worth

"While you were born with a self-worth and [it] is a gift of God to you to begin your life with, your net worth is what you build here on earth and what you choose to do with the resources and gifts that you have been given."

—Sunday Adelaja

PRINCIPLE 5:
Net Worth Is One Key Measure
of Financial Success—Debt Matters.

W hen asked to define money, most will immediately bring up the dollar bills in their wallet or the coins in the change jar on the kitchen counter at home. This is one way the word "money" is used in our common vernacular.

- Do you have enough *money* with you to afford that?
- He found some *money* behind the couch.
- He gave his granddaughter a birthday gift of *money*.

It's worth noting that all of these refer to *currency*, which is one form that money takes, but it's not the only form. In contrast to currency, money can also be defined as wealth, or value, which comes closer to the true meaning of it. *Merriam-Webster's Dictionary* defines money as "something generally accepted as a medium of exchange, measure of value, or means of payment."[6]

If we say that someone has a "lot of money," does that mean that he has a large pile of $100 bills at home? No, it simply means that he has a lot of *value* in all of the assets that he owns. In fact, *debt* must be included in this determination of money or worth. Someone may appear to own an expensive house, cars, clothing, and live a lavish lifestyle. But what if that lifestyle is propped up by significant debts that are owed on many, if not all, of those assets? Then that person certainly would not be considered *truly* wealthy. He would simply have the *appearance* of being wealthy.

Money or wealth can, therefore, more accurately be summed up in the term *net worth*. This is an accounting term, but don't let it put you off for that reason. Net worth simply means the sum of all of your assets (financial and physical) minus the sum of all of your debts. That's the concept we want to make as our core definition of money. This considers not only income and assets, but spending and debt. You can think of your net worth as the true scorecard for how well you are doing financially. If your *perception* of money—especially wealth—does not include debt, you are ignoring one of the most important factors in long-term financial success. There is a separate chapter on borrowing and debt later in the book, but for now I encourage you to consider it as a required component in the true calculation of your money and wealth.

This can help us weigh the actual financial status of any person or family. For example, someone may have significant financial assets—bank account balances, stocks, bonds, and Certificates of Deposit (CDs)—and may also have significant physical assets—house, land, cars, furniture, and tools. But if the value of all of their assets is matched by an equal amount of *debt*, then their net worth is zero! On the other hand, someone may have very modest financial and physical assets, worth $10,000 in total, but *no* debt at all. In this case, their net worth is $10,000. The first person has the *appearance* of wealth and a high net worth, but the second person actually *has* a higher net worth. We typically don't know the amount of debt that another person has accumulated. That is private and personal. But please note that unless you know someone's actual financial status, including their debts, you really don't know whether they are, in fact, wealthy or not.

Another way of understanding net worth is to visualize your heirs having to liquidate all of your assets after you have died. They would have to first take all of your financial assets—savings accounts, CDs, bonds, and stocks—and convert them to cash. Next, they would have an estate sale and sell, literally, all of your possessions, including your house and vehicles. They would then put the cash from that sale with the cash from your converted financial assets. Now, from this pool of funds, they must pay any outstanding debts and bills that you still have. After all debts are paid, what is left over? That is your net worth: the money left after liquidating all assets and paying all debts. If your debts are greater than your total liquidated assets, then you can be described as being "underwater" financially. That term is usually applied to a home loan, where the market value of the house is less than the outstanding debt that is owed. But it can apply to one's overall financial situation as well.

It is critically important to regularly calculate your net worth. If you have never done this before, you may be shocked at what you find. If you do a monthly calculation of this, which I recommend, then you will stay aware of this "bottom line" number that is so important. It will also become a helpful factor as you weigh whether to purchase something or not. At first, after buying a new car, for example, your net worth will remain unchanged. You pay $30,000 for a car, and you have a $30,000 car loan (assuming no down payment for our illustration), so they cancel each other out. But if the car depreciates faster than you are paying off the debt, your net worth may gradually be going *down* each month. You now owe more than the car is worth. Weighing this prospect may motivate you to put more money down on the car, or to even pay cash for it. (A car does go down in value though. It depreciates. So over time, your net worth with regard to vehicles slowly but steadily goes down.)

It is key to recognize that one true measure of financial success, of wealth, is your net worth. To the extent that your assets have debts associated with them, your net worth is diminished. Debt must be considered as well as assets owned in order to accurately assess wealth. Avoid the psychological trap that implies wealth is calculated by simply tallying up all of your assets, without including that all-important factor called *debt*.

Chapter 10

Principle of the Psychological Power of Money

"Don't think money does everything or you are going to end up doing everything for money."

—Voltaire

PRINCIPLE 6:
Money *Will* Influence You Psychologically.

Money, because of its very nature, has a psychological effect on everyone. For example, the absence of money can cause anxiety, fear, and stress. An abundance of money can result in the opposite effect: calmness rather than anxiety, confidence rather than fear, and peace rather than stress.

When a person doesn't have enough money, they feel a *loss of control* over their lives. Their lack prompts a realization that they don't have absolute choice in what they can and cannot do, or in what they might desire to do and purchase outside of their basic needs. They are constrained by what their money enables them to do.

The impact on the psyche when a person has money in a savings account versus having no savings plus debt can be profound. When you have enough savings to provide for yourself and your household for a few months if you lose your source of income, for example, there is a peace that comes with that knowledge.

Perhaps the greatest psychological impact is a fear that comes from the threat of not having enough money to pay all the regular bills and buy enough food to feed your family. To simply survive at the most basic level, a person needs enough money to pay for food, clothing, and shelter.

Money can psychologically warp our sense of values and priorities. Occasionally, someone will become so consumed with acquiring money that it becomes a goal in and of itself. Then, money is valued because of what it represents, both to the person acquiring it and to the world, who keeps score of these acquisitions. This can easily slip into greed, where there is always a desire for a bigger house, a newer car, and the latest in technology—basically, a continual desire to acquire more money.

In contrast to greed, another potential psychological response to having money is gratitude. Your attitude has a lot to do with how much you're able to enjoy financial success. If you hold it with a loose hand—with a grateful heart, as it were—freely delighting in blessing others, you, too, will be blessed by how you feel about your use of your money. But if you let yourself become greedy, then you will never have enough. You will become dissatisfied, unhappy, and fearful of losing your wealth. Your greed will rob you of the ability to enjoy what you have. Remember, success is not just owning the wealth; it's being able to enjoy wealth in a healthy manner.

The key here is to *be aware* of the psychological power of money. Recognize that it can have an influence on the way your mind and your heart work. If you know that and stay alert to guard against it, you will be better able to select and stick with your own financial path to success.

I encourage you to manage your thoughts about money; otherwise, money will manage your thoughts for you. What we think, we tend to do.

Chapter 11

Principle of Know Thyself

"Being wealthy isn't just a question of having lots of money. It's a question of what we want. Wealth isn't an absolute, it's relative to desire. Every time we seek something that we can't afford, we can be counted as poor, [regardless of] how much money we may actually have."

—Jean-Jacques Rousseau

PRINCIPLE 7:
You Must Understand Yourself
In Order to Know What You Need.

I n order to grow and advance in any discipline, you must know where you are starting from. That's as true about understanding and applying financial principles as it is about learning to play a musical instrument. Therefore, we must examine our attitudes and biases about money. "Know thyself" is as relevant today as it was when Plato stated it long ago.

It's important to recognize that we all may have some areas where our thinking about money is faulty or incorrect. But as long as we believe our thoughts are accurate and true, we will shape our actions accordingly. Only when you change your beliefs to align with truth can you then change your behavior so that it acts in accordance, and in harmony, with that truth.

As a starting point, I think we can agree that people are heavily influenced by the family in which they grew up. Therefore, you will probably tend to view money, and use money, very similarly to the way your parents or guardians did. This can be good if they had a correct, principle-based view of money. This can be bad if their view of money was incomplete or incorrect. Pause for a minute and reflect on how your parents, or other people involved in your upbringing, viewed money.

- Did your parents openly talk about money, or did they not discuss money at all?

- Were they thrifty?
- Did your parents convey a sense that your family had enough money? Or was the opposite true?
- Were your parents honest in their monetary dealings with others?
- Were they generous?
- Did you feel like your family was poor?

Now ask yourself how many of their perceptions and beliefs you see in your own life. Probably at least some of them were absorbed and have become a part of the way you see the world. The challenge is to be able to step back from those perceptions and examine them to see if they stand up to scrutiny and if they are based on fact. At this point, I'm just asking you to be open to questioning them. Are they really true, or are they a misconception that you absorbed? We must accept the fact that we might have some blind spots regarding money.

We each have areas where we are weaker in our resolve to manage our financial lives well. Often, this is in the form of spending—purchasing retail items, such as clothing, cars, furniture, or expensive toys. Or it could be a weakness toward experiences, such as regularly going to the movies or theater, or taking frequent vacations. Our weakness with spending can be in any category. The key is to honestly assess and understand *your* weaknesses so that you can be alert to their influence on you.

Take a minute and reflect on the following questions about your views regarding finances.

- What are your personal thoughts about money?
- Do you feel that you use money wisely?
- How do you define financial success?

- Do you know what your net worth is?
- What is your level of knowledge about earning, saving, spending, and investing?

There are no right or wrong answers here. The point is for you to identify your personal views and actions regarding money, then weigh how well your finances have worked out based on them. If you have not been successful in your management of your financial life, I challenge you to reflect on *why* you have not been successful. Do you need more financial education? Do you have low self-esteem? Are you undisciplined? It can be any number of things. The key is to become *self-aware* of where you need help so that you can focus on those areas.

Be encouraged! You are intelligent and can absorb and learn how to apply proven financial concepts and practices no matter how much or how little formal education you have had—even if you struggled to succeed in many of your classes in school. You're limited only by your preconceived notions of what you can or can't do.

In order to overcome your weaknesses with regard to managing your finances, you must first know what those weaknesses are. You won't change your behavior until you change your thinking. You won't change your thinking until you become convinced that your thinking is faulty and unproductive, perhaps even counterproductive. If you understand your current personal views on money, then you can better avoid falling into mind traps ("thinking errors") due to your personal weaknesses.

Principles About How We Use Money

N ow we're ready for the heart of the principles—how we actually *use* money in our lives. These are the areas that typically come to mind when someone mentions financial management. We will review the six key topics of earning, spending, borrowing, saving, investing, and giving. These will be discussed individually, but we'll also examine how they are related and how they can impact one another.

Chapter 12

Principle of Earning

"The more you learn, the more you earn."

—Frank A. Clark

PRINCIPLE 8:
You Must First Earn Before You Can Save.

I n order to have money, you must first acquire it. For most of us that means we must earn it through working at a job, either at a company with a boss, or by becoming an entrepreneur. It's true that you could win the lottery, hit the jackpot at the casino, or inherit a fortune from a distant rich uncle. But these are not very likely, and certainly can't be counted on as sources of income. Therefore, in order to be successful, we must learn how to maximize the income we receive from our working career.

Some shy away from the term "career," believing that it carries the connotation of slaving away in a large corporation where the worker becomes just a cog in a giant machine. I believe that "career" can be a useful description for whatever means a person chooses to earn an income, and I invite you to think of it in that same way. It can encompass everything from being a doctor, a factory worker, or a welder, to a writer, a teacher, or an entrepreneur—and everything in between.

This is an important choice. You will spend the largest percentage of your waking hours engaged in your career. So it's worth spending some time to research and determine what options seem to be the best fit for you.

Recognize that a job also provides much more than a source of funds for you and your family to live on. Your career, the right career, can provide you with many satisfying things.

- The pleasure of doing something you enjoy
- The camaraderie of working together with others on a common goal
- The pride of developing increasing skill in something worthwhile
- Being respected for what you know and do
- The satisfaction of helping others achieve their life goals
- An opportunity to learn, to grow, and to become more than you ever imagined

To get from not having a career to having an established career requires several steps, regardless of the career being pursued. Let's examine those steps to see what we can learn. In this chapter we will look at the following stages of career development:

1) Choosing a career
2) Getting the education needed to prepare for a specific career
3) Maximizing the opportunities for getting the best job available in your chosen career field
4) Succeeding in a career
5) Changing careers: what to do when it doesn't work out!

1) Choosing a Career

First of all, it should be noted that there are literally thousands of different careers available today. With the explosion of advancements in technology, communications, manufacturing, and transportation, there are many more opportunities available now than there ever were for previous generations.

If you had lived two hundred years ago, your opportunities would have been far more limited. Think with me for a minute about what careers or crafts might have been an option for you at that time. You could have been a farmer, carpenter, mason, shop owner, or banker. You could have become an attorney, doctor, baker, tailor, blacksmith, rancher, or sailor. And the final options might have been shipping merchant, prospector, sheriff, government worker, printing press operator, or general laborer. That would essentially be the complete list of available careers! It was very common for a young man to simply follow in the footsteps of his father, and perhaps even grandfather, in his career choice. Very few occupations were available to women—teacher, nurse, seamstress, social worker, and perhaps singer or dancer. Not much else. Most were homemakers and did not pursue a career as such. Today, there are so many career options for both men and women that it can be overwhelming to someone when deciding what path to pursue. The challenge for someone today is not so much finding a career as it is *whittling down* the plethora of career opportunities to a shorter list of really good candidates for them as an individual.

One thing to note here is that there could easily be a dozen or more occupations that we would each find acceptable. Without a doubt, multiple rivers all lead to the same sea, and there are many, many ways to earn an income. Any of them could probably provide a decent wage with good working conditions and allow you to utilize your talents and skills. The first challenge, then, is to narrow all of the career options down to a short list of good candidates. Next, do a careful, realistic assessment of each of them in terms of the pay received, the expected demand for that field, and the suitability of the job as a match for your personal interests, passions, and talents.

This research can require an investment of time and effort, and for some this step gets shuffled to the back of their priority list. If you could be happy doing any of a dozen occupations, though, why not seek to find the one or two that will pay the most, have the greatest demand for future employment, and be the best fit for you in terms of the work required? Yet so much of the time, people simply fall into something, acquire some competence, and then stay in it until retirement. There is very little thought given to what is available, what their skills are, what their talents are, the pay scales of different careers, and where they might have to live in order to get a job in a given field.

How is one to choose among the many occupations available today? The first step is to learn about yourself. What are your talents, skills, passions, and preferences? High school or college placement centers and guidance counselors are a good resource to tap for suggestions and ideas on learning about yourself. There are several vocational interest tests available that can give you an idea of your aptitudes and interests. The Strong Interest Inventory® test is a good example, but there are many others. These tests will also determine and list those careers that are recognized as being a potential fit for your particular combination of talents and interests. There are also a number of excellent printed resources available on the subject, some of which are included in the Further Reading list at the end of this book. One in particular that many have found to be helpful is *What Color Is Your Parachute?* by Richard Bolles. It was originally published in 1970 but has been revised annually since 1975 with new and updated material to keep it relevant. It is now available in twenty-two languages and is sold in twenty-six countries.

Over ten million copies have been sold to date, attesting to its popularity.

After learning more about yourself and your natural abilities, the next step is to find those careers that would be a good fit. As mentioned earlier, when you take one or more of the vocational interest tests they will typically provide a list of occupations that appear to be the best match for you. Then, from that list, you can do more detailed research into those that sound interesting. Some aspects to explore could include educational requirements, average salary, expected future growth in the demand for that field, and any location or travel requirements.

A word about salary. You must choose a career that is satisfying and rewarding to you, but it's also prudent to do some research to see which career fields pay well and which do not. It's probably true that you could be happy in several different careers. If that's true, and you can determine what those half-dozen careers are, then it would be good to find out how plentiful the jobs are in the market for each career, and also find out how much typical jobs pay. Then you can make your decision on which ones to pursue further, recognizing the tradeoffs that you're deliberately choosing to make between career appeal and expected income.

To get a practical perspective on any of them, I recommend interviewing someone currently in each of those careers. Most people would be happy to give you a few minutes of their time to explain what they do for a living. Hopefully, they enjoy their work and will be pleased to see someone else considering entering that field. Be sure to prepare a list of questions beforehand in order to make the best use of your time with them. Some possible questions to consider:

- What is a typical day in your profession like?
- What do you most enjoy about your job?
- What do you most dislike about your job?
- What preparation would you recommend in order to be successful in this career?
- Is there much travel involved?
- Do you work primarily in an office, from home, or do you typically work outdoors?

An internship is a great way to get a feel for what day-to-day life is like in an occupation. Some internships primarily involve paperwork or menial tasks, but the best ones give you a chance to learn more about the true "nuts and bolts" of that job. Those are the internships to look for. The career counseling office at the local college is a great place to check for internship opportunities.

2) Getting the Education Needed to Prepare for a Specific Career

Once you have decided on a career, now you must seek the best education available. You want to acquire the knowledge and skills needed to be successful in your chosen field. You must research colleges, trade schools, or other educational providers to determine which ones offer an excellent preparation for you, as well as which offer the best value for the money.

A comment here about paying for your education. Student debt has ballooned over the past twenty years and is now the second largest form of debt in the US, second only to mortgage debt. As mentioned in chapter 1, "Americans now owe more than $1.75 trillion in student loan debt, based on the most current figures available to Nitro."[7] This will be discussed in more detail in the chapter on debt, but it still warrants mentioning here. You must adopt the mindset that you will do everything possible to avoid, or at least minimize, student debt. As you're considering colleges, your research needs to include how much the education will cost. A degree from a prestigious school may look good on a résumé, but is it going to be worth the additional cost? There will be educational opportunities available at widely varying price points. Just keep that in mind as you do your research.

Once you have been accepted and have begun your education, it's important to do the very best that you can. The better your grades, the more opportunities you will have available to you when you graduate. Keep in mind that companies also look for candidates that are well-rounded and not just technically skilled. Participating in extracurricular activities is therefore often viewed favorably by companies when they are interviewing candidates.

3) Maximizing the Opportunities for Getting the Best Job Available in Your Chosen Career Field

As you are wrapping up your education, how do you find, and get hired by, the best company or organization—the one that will offer the best opportunities for your career? This is the time for you to put on your researcher hat and dig into what is involved in getting hired. You must learn what to do in order to find the best companies, then learn how to present yourself in the best light possible. Skills such as writing a résumé, participating in an interview, and following recommended courtesies when communicating with a company are all important. Even learning the most appropriate way to dress is helpful and often overlooked. College placement centers have ample information available on everything related to job hunting. Their resource libraries can include significant online resources, but you can also find valuable information in the books, brochures, videos, or in-person classes they have on hand. They want you to succeed in your job search, so they provide what they believe would be helpful to you. I encourage you to take advantage of these free resources to prepare yourself as thoroughly as possible. There may be many people applying for the available positions in which you are interested. You want to present your "best face" to the interviewer and the company to maximize your chances of getting hired.

A word of advice here: I recommend that you start looking early in the fall if you're graduating in the spring. Many companies do their primary interviewing in the fall for those graduating the following May. If you wait until spring to start your job search, a lot of the available jobs may already have been taken. Don't wait. Resources are available to help you in this search. The college placement office will have information about companies that typically recruit at that school. Vocational training schools will also have a list of companies that often hire from their pool of students.

As you are researching and developing your interviewing skills, you will also need to research the companies and job opportunities available in the area where you wish to work. For those graduating from college, the placement office is a great place to start. Companies that interview at that college will typically provide information about their job offerings to the placement center. The Internet is perhaps one of your best sources of information about companies you're considering. Search for each company by name, absorbing and recording the key facts about each of them. Gradually, you will begin to develop a feel for the primary companies you wish to consider and the advantages and disadvantages of each. Be sure to participate in job fairs or other similar opportunities to meet company representatives.

I encourage you to aim high. Try to find the very best job at the best company in the career field you're pursuing. Don't just settle for whatever might be available after a brief search. Keep looking until you uncover some great companies. Be willing to move to a different city or area of the country. Doing so will make you a candidate for a wider pool of jobs.

In evaluating companies and job openings, here are some things to look for:

- They offer an excellent training program.
- They value efficient organization, even in their recruiting process.
- Their staff are happy and fulfilled employees. (Check glassdoor.com for employee ratings.)
- The company is financially successful.
- They have a good reputation.
- They deliver a product or service that you like and feel is worthwhile.
- You would be proud to work there.
- The personality of the company seems to be a good fit for you.

Asking instructors (especially those in your major) for their suggestions can be productive. Many companies will establish and maintain regular contact with the professors in the fields for which they are recruiting.

4) Succeeding in a Career

Now that you have that dream job, how do you succeed at it? What do you need to do to maximize your income over your working life? Again, there are many books, podcasts, instructor-led classes, user groups, and instructional materials available to help in this regard.

Let me offer a few suggestions.

First of all, there are what I will call "general job skills." These are things that you begin to learn while working your first job as a teenager, perhaps flipping burgers at McDonald's. These skills are not oriented toward any particular career, but rather to working at any job. To be an outstanding employee, I recommend doing *at least* the following things:

- Be industrious (often described as being a "hard worker").
- Be optimistic and helpful.
- Be reliable.
- Be punctual.
- Dress appropriately.
- Focus on delivering results, not just putting in the expected hours.
- Be willing to make some sacrifices—for example, working late occasionally as needed.
- Look for opportunities to do more in your current job, such as volunteering for tasks.
- When you make a mistake, own up to it, then learn what you need to do so you don't make that mistake again.

In addition to these general job skills, the other thing you must do is research what *specific* skills are valued in your chosen career. It may be skills in communication, such as the ability to teach classes. It could be a set of technical abilities unique to your chosen career. It might even be flexibility, such as willingness to travel or work odd shifts. You must work to learn what it takes to succeed in your specific profession or craft. This is one that you will have to figure out on your own. Remember, all of your coworkers are also interested in succeeding, and they will be trying to figure out the same things you are. To some extent, your success will depend upon your accurate assessment of what is required to succeed at your job. Sometimes it may be *who* you know, not *what* you know. In the best companies, though, advancement and promotions will be based on fair, objective criteria. If you feel that your company plays favorites and ignores the quality of work people are doing, you have two choices. You can either decide to play office politics and "suck up" to the boss, just like everyone else, or look for a different company and a different job—one that treats their employees fairly.

You must continually educate yourself on the latest changes, trends, and demands of your job, as well as continue to sharpen and hone your job skills. If you are with a good company, your outstanding work will be recognized and rewarded. Promotions, pay raises, and new opportunities will be the results of your efforts.

One final point about succeeding on the job is to be careful not to sacrifice your enjoyment of the job in the process of becoming financially successful. Perhaps the most common example of this is when a technical professional, such as an engineer, moves up into management and finds that they are no longer solving engineering problems themselves, but rather they are directing others as they solve those problems. Some people find management to be an enjoyable challenge. Others hate it. Therefore, if you think you will dislike being in management, you may want to decline that opportunity, even though it might pay more than you make as an engineer.

5) Changing Careers: What to Do When It Doesn't Work Out!

You may find that, in spite of your best efforts, your chosen career is not a good fit for you. This could be due to a variety of reasons, most of them unique to you. Some careers are less desirable in general, but for the most part, a career is pleasurable because it's a good fit for your personality, temperament, and skillset.

Before jumping ship and changing jobs or careers, it's important to recognize that every job will have some aspects about it which you may find to be boring, tedious, or distasteful. You don't want to hop from job to job, or from career to career, though, looking for that elusive "perfect" job. You could waste a lifetime doing that if you aren't careful.

The focus of this chapter is on *earning*, so I would be remiss if I didn't note that, when you follow your heart, you may not end up with a career that nets you the greatest income. There are plenty of jobs that are exciting, adventurous, and rewarding, but the pay is not so great. But—and this is an important "but"—if you are doing what you love, that goes a long way toward providing lifetime happiness. It may be a bit of a tradeoff, but job satisfaction is crucial; high pay is optional.

If you have decided to change course and try a different career, I suggest that you cycle back through the steps outlined above regarding learning about the available jobs, the education required, and how to position yourself to succeed. It isn't that uncommon for people to change careers, especially given how much careers themselves change over time. Just don't leave your old job without paving the way for the new one first. Figure out what you need to do, then begin preparing yourself through continuing education or learning new skills while you remain in your current job and keep your source of income.

Earning money is the first step in establishing a good financial plan. You can't spend or save what you don't have, so you must acquire money before you have any options available regarding what to do with it. The career you choose will largely determine your lifetime income, so think about both job satisfaction and typical income levels when evaluating a career. Finally, doing the best you can at the job you already have is an important factor in achieving success.

Chapter 13

Principle of Spending

"Caveat emptor. [Let the buyer beware.]"

—Latin proverb

PRINCIPLE 9:
If You Spend Wisely,
You Get More for Your Money.

Money exists only for the purpose of ultimately being spent, either in the present or in the future. Money, wealth, and a large bank account, in and of themselves, do not mean anything outside of the buying power they impart to their owner. Spending is important. It has a purpose. In order to live in harmony with the principle related to spending money, though, you must understand the value of items to be purchased, and then spend wisely.

Spending is an area where many people struggle. You can *always* find more things to spend your money on than the amount of money you have. Retailers don't make it any easier for the consumer, as they are always working to encourage you to spend more. Consider for a moment that consumer spending is the major source of gross domestic product in the United States. Approximately two-thirds of the total revenue generated by all businesses in this country comes from purchases by individual consumers like you and me. The upshot of this is that companies are competing for your attention and, ultimately, for your hard-earned dollars. There is an entire business discipline labeled "marketing" whose sole purpose is maximizing the selling of a company's products or services. You can even specialize your education and get a bachelor's or master's degree in marketing. Some firms exist solely to help other companies advertise and market themselves to the world. Everywhere you look, you are bombarded with advertising—on TV, on the Internet, on billboards, on social media, and in flyers you receive in the mail.

I mention all of this to remind you that the true purpose of marketing is not to inform you; it is to induce you to buy a product or service. It is certainly true that advertising often does help you understand how a product works and the advantages it may offer over its competitors. But never forget: they are trying to *sell* you something. Keep your guard up.

So how can you spend wisely? What steps or techniques are helpful to utilize in accomplishing that? I have outlined below several suggestions for your consideration.

Decide if You Really Need It

It may seem obvious, but the first and most effective way to manage your spending is to forgo some purchases. If you decide you really don't need something and then don't buy it, you have just eliminated that expense completely. Remember, as a buyer, you always have the option to choose not to purchase something.

Let Income Determine Spending

We are about to discuss here what I believe is the most important advice in this book. You will even find it discussed again in the chapter on savings because it impacts both areas so significantly. I cannot overstate the importance of understanding this one basic concept. If you get nothing else out of this book, following this guideline will dramatically improve your financial life. I guarantee it.

Spend less than you make.

"But that's impossible!" you might say. "I have all of these things that I need. If I spend less than I make, I will have to live like a pauper!" And right away, we find ourselves at the crux of the matter. What I want you to think about, mull over, and hopefully understand is the tradeoff you're making when you spend more than you make. This advice goes hand in hand with the principle of borrowing, which will be discussed in greater detail in the next chapter. The core truth here is that the only way you can spend more than you make is if you borrow to make up the difference.

When you borrow, you begin paying interest to the one who loaned you the funds. Now you are paying a premium for whatever you purchased. You are not only paying the price of the item to the seller; on top of that, you are paying the one who loaned you the funds. This can dramatically increase the cost of whatever you're buying. All of the money you pay as interest cannot be used for anything else. It cannot be saved. It cannot be used to buy something different. It is gone, never to return.

Spending less than you make may require a radical rethinking on your part. You must wrestle with the decision regarding the standard of living that you *choose* to maintain. This is primarily of greatest impact in the early years of a person's working life when their income is much lower. Spending less will likely mean you will have to decrease your standard of living, perhaps significantly. That could include the house or apartment in which you live, the car you drive, the clothes you wear, and virtually every other area of your life. Does it mean you must live this way forever? Not at all. But if you carefully control your spending at this stage of your life, it will allow you to do two wonderful things: 1) pay off your debt, and 2) begin saving. Over time, as you receive pay increases, you will then be able to gradually increase your standard of living while still being able to add to your savings and be generous to others.

If you become convinced that it would be good for you to adopt this approach, remember that you must consider the power of habit. Psychologists tell us that it takes thirty days to break an old habit or form a new one. That means even after you have resolved to decrease your spending by spending less than you earn, your old habit will keep pushing you to revert back to your former spending habits, your old way of thinking. You must be doggedly determined to stick with any change for more than thirty days before the power of habit can begin to help you rather than pull you down. It may also take several weeks to weigh and implement changes in your lifestyle. It will not be easy, but it's worth the struggle. If this area is a tough one for you, please refer back to the earlier chapter on habit for more details and suggestions regarding the principle of habit and how to deal with it.

The way you spend today, tomorrow, and next week is setting a pattern for the way you will spend for the rest of your life. A common piece of wisdom is that the definition of insanity is doing the same thing over and over again and expecting different results. There's a lot of truth in that little saying. If you don't change your pattern of spending today, or this week, then when will you? If you don't choose to change, then this pattern will continue on into later adulthood, and even into retirement. It becomes a way of life for you to be in debt. It feels normal. But you *can* change that. You can begin today to rewrite the story of your life, if you choose.

Plan Your Spending

Many people find it helpful to *plan* what they spend, and this typically takes the form of a budget. There are many approaches available to help with budgeting and managing your spending. These can be as simple as the "envelope" approach, where you buy exclusively with cash, keeping your budgeted amount for each category in a separate envelope. When that envelope is empty, you don't spend any more in that category until your next payday, when you refill all of your envelopes. Many of the most common budget systems are in the form of a software package, which can provide a more automated approach. I have included in the Further Reading section a link to an Investopedia article that reviewed many of the most popular packages, assessing the advantages of each and then offering their recommendations. I have personally used YNAB (or You Need A Budget) and EveryDollar, and they both work well. All of the packages offer a different mix of features and strengths. The key is to find a plan that fits you so it can be a help to you rather than a burden. If you try to use a budgeting system you hate, you won't stick with it. Budgeting should not be a burdensome process. It is simply a way of helping you spend money on what's important to you, as well as helping you stay within the "guard rails" of how much you have to spend. If you're comfortable using spreadsheets, you can also just create your own budgeting and tracking plan. I have found that to work well also.

Many financial advisers recommend aiming to set aside money for savings as the first amount that's taken out of your paycheck. This is sometimes referred to as "paying yourself" before you pay anyone else. This helps confirm to yourself each month that saving is a priority. If you believe in tithing, I suggest that you take this category out even before savings. As far as how much to set aside, I suggest tithing or donating 10 percent, saving 15 percent, then using the rest to live on. You may not be able to jump to this level of giving and saving immediately. Most people find that if they can start in that direction by giving 1 percent and saving 1 percent, then increasing the percentage each year, or each time they get a pay raise, they can eventually get to 10 percent giving and 15 percent saving. If you have debt, other than a mortgage, you may want to pay your debt down first, since you will almost certainly be paying a far higher interest rate on your debt than you will earn on your savings.

Buy Quality

Once you have decided how much to spend on something, you want to maximize the value that you get for your money. This involves researching what product options are available and trying to assess which product offers the highest quality for the best price. Reading product reviews helps with this. References such as *Consumer Reports* can also be useful. Assessing the stability and reputation of a brand should also give some indication of the typical quality found in products of that brand.

It's important to determine what features are important to you. Many products come in a variety of models, with varying degrees of functionality. You want to avoid paying for extra features that you will likely not use. Buying used products is a strategy that can net significant savings, particularly on automobiles.

Maintain What You Buy

Once you have purchased something, it is wise to properly maintain it. Some items require almost no maintenance at all, such as a hair dryer, for example. Others require significant maintenance, such as a house, car, boat, motorcycle, or computer. If you don't change the oil regularly on a gasoline engine, it will not last as long or perform as well.

Have Some Fun Money

I would suggest that in your spending budget you set aside some funds as "fun money." It's human nature to want to purchase something occasionally simply because you want it, even though you really don't need it. It might even be a seemingly unwise decision based on how much you're paying for it and considering its value in the marketplace. If it gives you joy, though, and it's not too expensive, it is okay to buy it just because you want it. If you allow yourself to splurge occasionally on small things, it will help you to resist splurging on bigger-ticket items, where the overall cost to you is much greater, and potentially more damaging.

Beware the Power of Marketing

Keep your shield and your guard up against skillful marketing. Educate yourself on some of the most common ways that companies market their products, which are often subtle and not obvious at all. When marketing materials seem to gush about how much this product or service will do for you, remember to ask in the back of your mind what it does for the *seller*.

Here are just a few marketing strategies companies use to entice you to purchase. There are, of course, many more.

- Impulse buying—displaying candy next to the checkout line
- Appealing to your sense of entitlement
- "You deserve a break today" (a jingle from an old McDonald's advertisement)

- Follow the crowd—convincing you that everyone else is buying it
- Today-only special—plays on your FOMO ("fear of missing out")
- Natural—by describing something as "natural," it appeals to our desire to live healthy
- Feel good—they give you a comforting feeling
  - Is Starbucks' coffee really any better than anyone else's? In blind taste tests, volunteers often preferred the taste and flavor of Dunkin' Donuts over Starbucks. But what does Starbucks offer? A warm, cozy, "coffee shop" ambience, exotic names for their drinks (not a "large," but a "venti"), and the invitation to customize your drink, thus making your purchase something that has been personally crafted to suit your unique, special desires.

Perhaps the best (or worst) example of powerful marketing is attending a sales presentation with a room full of other potential customers. When you do this, you're placing yourself in the hands of some of the most skillful and practiced marketers and sales people in the country. They are experts, who are often so persuasive that you come away feeling privileged that you were able to buy something from them.

I once attended such a seminar in Branson, Missouri, that was a sales presentation for vacation timeshares. I had felt that I was pretty resistant to sales tactics, but I ended up buying a timeshare in spite of that. (Let me pause and note that some people have timeshares and are completely happy and satisfied with them. Not everyone dislikes timeshares.)

When I got home, I sat down and spent the next day carefully reading over all the material that I had received as part of the purchase. It became increasingly clear to me that this was not a good deal for my family for several reasons. Perhaps the strongest was that you couldn't cancel your timeshare. The obligation to make the regular payments would even be passed on to your heirs after you died! It was perpetual. As a consumer, I knew I had three days, by law, to back out of the contract. So before that deadline was reached, I prepared a letter canceling my purchase and mailed it via certified mail to the address indicated so I would have proof that they received my cancelation.

Interestingly, even though I canceled that contract years ago, I still occasionally receive phone calls from various companies offering to help me get out of my timeshare. It seems that the timeshare industry has spawned another related industry devoted exclusively to helping people get out of them!

Spending is the most common financial trap. Our emotions can betray us, thwarting all good plans and intentions. We must consciously plan what to spend and then stick to our plan. Give yourself some little playful luxuries to satisfy that desire to splurge within you. This desire must be satisfied, at least in some way, or it will rear its ugly head and drag you into big, painful purchases you will later regret. Guard against it with dogged tenacity. Stay alert to marketing strategies. Remember that their overriding purpose is to separate you from your money—to sell you something.

Chapter 14

Principle of Borrowing

"Money is a great servant but a bad master."

—Francis Bacon

PRINCIPLE 10:
The Borrower Is Slave to the Lender.

B orrowing and being in debt has become an embedded part of American culture. It has become the norm to have debt. Although not often discussed with family, friends, and coworkers, it is likely that many of them have debt, perhaps significant debt. It is likely that *you* have debt. Consumer debt reached $14.56 trillion after the fourth quarter of 2020, according to the New York Federal Reserve. The largest components of this were mortgages, student debt, and credit card debt. Non-housing debt has risen the fastest, increasing 51 percent since 2013.[8] The average interest rate being paid was a staggering 14.52 percent![9] For some households this is very manageable, but for many others, it is a crushing burden that they struggle to get out from under.

What is borrowing, exactly? The *Cambridge Dictionary* defines it as "to get or receive something from someone with the intention of giving it back after a period of time."[10] An alternate, more financially-oriented definition they provide is "to take money from a bank or other financial organization and pay it back over a period of time."[11] The key factor is that it must be returned. It must be paid back. It actually isn't *yours*. Unless you get a loan from a generous parent or relative, there will also be interest applied to the amount that must be repaid. This is the fee that is required for the privilege of using someone else's money for a period of time. This is fair, since they can't use that money for anything else while it's in your possession.

Is borrowing good or bad? It can be either, depending upon many factors. Borrowing, in and of itself, is not inherently bad. It is simply a tool, and, as with most tools, you must use it properly to get the greatest benefit from it. It's generally considered an appropriate approach when you are borrowing to purchase an asset that will appreciate, or increase, in value. The most common example of this would be borrowing in order to buy a house.

There are other situations where borrowing is not such a good idea. One common example of this would be using a credit card to buy a luxury item with the idea of paying it off over time when your household is struggling to simply pay the monthly bills.

To determine whether borrowing in a situation is good or bad, you must examine *how much* is being borrowed, *why* it is being borrowed, and what are the *terms*? For example, getting a mortgage (a home loan) is usually a good strategy. But even then, if you buy a bigger house than you can afford, and have a mortgage payment that stretches your family budget to the limit, this otherwise good strategy has now become a toxic one due to excessive borrowing.

The same can be true for buying a car. Early in your working career, you may need to borrow to purchase a car for general transportation when you don't have enough savings yet to be able to buy it outright. Therefore, borrowing in this case can be considered a good approach. But if you choose to buy an expensive car, with many more features than you need, your car payments will be quite a bit higher, and the impact on your budget will be significant. This is probably not a good decision.

I have been as prone to making financial missteps regarding debt as anyone else. In my younger days, I always seemed to have several debts I was paying on—credit cards, car loans, home improvement loans, and medical bills. This went on for quite a few years, as perhaps it has for you. We are all susceptible to the instant availability of credit and to the eventual outlook that using it is unavoidable.

Borrowing serves the important purpose of enabling a purchase to be made that would otherwise be impossible. If an entrepreneur wants to start or expand a business, he or she may very likely need to borrow the funds to do that, with the expectation that the revenue from the expanded capacity will enable the loan to be repaid and generate extra income over and above the loan payments, including interest.

Perhaps the most important factor in dealing successfully with credit is how you think about borrowing. Do you just take it for granted as a part of life? Do you expect to always be in debt? Or do you have a desire, *and a plan*, for steadily working your way out of debt? My hope is that, in this chapter, I can give you some things to think about and perhaps cause you to reconsider how you use debt.

Let's review and assess some of the more common types of borrowing.

Buying a Home

For most families, buying a home usually involves borrowing, commonly known as obtaining a mortgage. This allows the household to purchase an asset that will both provide them a place to live, a home base, and will also be an investment that (usually) appreciates in value. This is typically a worthwhile use of borrowing.

Student Debt

Taking on student debt in order to get a college degree has become commonplace. On the face of it, this appears to be a good thing. The loan enables the student to pay for college, get a degree, and thereby be equipped to perform a much higher-paying job than without the degree. Unfortunately, the cost for a college education has been going up much faster than the inflation rate. "For the 2018–19 academic year, annual current dollar prices for undergraduate tuition, fees, room, and board were estimated to be $18,383 at public institutions, $47,419 at private nonprofit institutions, and $27,040 at private for-profit institutions. Between 2008–09 and 2018–19, prices for undergraduate tuition, fees, room, and board at public institutions rose 28 percent, and prices at private nonprofit institutions rose 19 percent, after adjustment for inflation."[12] The sad truth is that many students graduate with a staggering amount of debt that may take twenty or more years to pay off. A student loan *can* be a good thing but only if it doesn't become too big and burdensome.

Credit Cards

Perhaps the most pervasive form of borrowing in today's economy is through the use of credit cards. They provide a purchase experience that is fast, easy, and smooth. Nearly every major retail business offers a branded credit card that grants the customer some additional benefits, such as frequent shopper points or the opportunity to participate in special sales. Many shoppers have multiple credit cards and may carry a case designed specifically for holding ten, fifteen, or more credit cards. It's now viewed as the standard way to live.

Credit cards can be handy indeed. If you pay off your balance in full every month, before the due date, there is typically no cost to you for using the card. This gives you a grace period, usually up to thirty days, to pay for a product that you purchased with the card. They will send you a statement each month that details every purchase you made. Card companies often have other perks as well, such as travel insurance if you pay for your trip with the card. They will alert you to fraudulent use of your card and notify you if there is any suspicious activity in your account. These are all tremendous benefits and cost you nothing—*if you pay off your card in full each month.*

The credit card companies, as you probably surmised, would likely not be able to stay in business if all customers did this. They are offering a financial service to you and, to provide that, it requires employees, offices, computers, and all of the other assets needed to run a business. The way they earn revenue is by charging interest on the balance you carry on your card from month to month, and by charging the merchants a percentage of each sale. Their rates are not cheap. As mentioned in an earlier chapter, in 2020, "the average interest rate being paid [by consumers] was 14.52%."[13] That is a very good return, *for the credit card companies,* on the money you borrowed from them when you charged a purchase and let the balance carry forward.

It's interesting to note that credit cards did not become available until the 1950s. Prior to that, if you wished to borrow money, you either visited your local bank or hit up your friend or family member. I have included a reference to an excellent article on the history of credit cards in the Further Reading section at the end of the book. In spite of what we might think, credit cards are a relatively recent development.

Borrowing from Family

Another type of borrowing would be from a family member or friend, with the expectation of paying zero or very little interest. This probably happens in many families, and it can certainly be a helpful boost to get you over a rough patch. I borrowed from relatives myself in the early years of my working career, and those loans enabled us to make some home improvements that could not have otherwise been afforded. The risk is that, if the loan is not repaid in the manner that all parties are expecting, hard feelings can result. This can become a wedge that drives apart close friends or family members. If you choose to borrow from someone in this way, I recommend that you draw up a promissory note, outlining all payments, their due dates, the interest rate to be paid, and any other unique facts about the loan. Then, be sure to send the payment every month, on time, just as you would any other debt. Don't take advantage of the good relationship you have by being sloppy or negligent in paying it off. If you do, you may lose a friend or cause a rift with a family member. Not to mention that you will most certainly lose the opportunity to ever borrow from them again!

Predatory Lending

A brief comment about predatory lending is needed. This group of lenders preys upon those who, for various reasons, may not be able to get a loan from anyone else. It includes payday lending, pawn shops, loan sharks, and anyone else who provides this type of loan. The borrower is usually a poor credit risk and may not be able to repay the loan at all, so there is a high risk of them defaulting on it. As a result, the interest rates are ridiculously high.

In a 2021 article in *Bloomberg News*, they calculated that one payday lending customer was paying 589 percent interest with payments due every two weeks, and that was considered fairly typical for payday lending.[14] In the case of defaulting on a pawn shop loan, the borrower also sacrifices the article that they pawned. My advice would be to avoid these lenders at all cost. They are offering a legal service, but they are capitalizing on someone else's lack of financial acumen, poor financial management skills, and desperate situation.

Borrowing Pros and Cons

The advantage of borrowing in general is that you get funds immediately. If you can't wait to save up to pay for something, borrowing provides an alternative to waiting.

There are, however, significant disadvantages to borrowing.

- You may pay high interest rates.
- It takes money that could be used for savings.
- You are a "slave" to the lender in that you are legally obligated to repay the debt.
- It requires being careful to make each monthly payment on time. If you are late, or miss a payment, a penalty fee is applied, and your interest rate will also go up, perhaps dramatically. This is a continual financial sword hanging over you and is stressful.
- You are helping someone else make money at your expense.

In general, it is much better *not* to borrow money. When you borrow, the person or company you are borrowing from is putting their money to work, and you are paying them for it!

Working Your Way Out of Debt

There are several approaches to working your way out of credit card and other consumer debt. One that I favor and recommend is known as the "snowball" approach. To use it, you make a list of all of the debts that you have, excluding only your home mortgage. Determine the minimum monthly payment that each requires, and begin paying only the minimum for each debt except for the one with the smallest balance. Any extra that you can put toward paying off your debts should be added to the minimum charge for that smallest debt. As soon as the smallest debt is paid off, take the amount that you were paying toward that debt and add it to the minimum payment for the debt with the next largest balance. This enables the amount you're paying off to continue to get larger, like a rolling snowball, every time you pay off one debt and roll to the next one. Continue this process until all credit card debts are paid off, finishing up with the largest one. It's important to strive to not incur any *new* credit card debt while you're paying it down. The advantage of the snowball approach is primarily psychological. When you're able to quickly pay off smaller debts, it's an encouraging boost to your feeling of accomplishment and keeps you motivated to continue your debt repayment plan.

Another approach to paying off debt is to first focus on those debts that have the highest interest rates. This concept is similar to the snowball approach in that any extra funds go to paying off *one* specific debt, then when it is paid off, the one with the next highest interest rate is addressed. Many like this approach, and if that appeals to you, then I encourage you to use it. It has the advantage of eliminating the most expensive debts first, in terms of the interest rate being paid. The downside is that your most expensive debts may be the largest. This will mean that all of your other debts, and their required minimum payments, may continue for quite some time, which can be discouraging.

Borrowing Tips

Here are a few final suggestions about borrowing wisely:

- Research your options—interest rates and terms may vary.
- Be diligent about paying on time every month. You will, thereby, avoid being charged a penalty fee and having your interest rate jump up.
- Demonstrate that you are responsible about repaying your debt, and your credit score will gradually go up. Your credibility will also go up, should you ever need to borrow again.
- Read the fine print. I once applied for a credit card that stated in the contract details that they could raise my interest rate if I was late on paying *any* debts, with *any* creditors, not just with this particular card company. I wrote them a letter asking if they could offer the card without that requirement, and surprisingly they sent me back new terms without that language in it!
- Pay off your credit card balance in full each month, and you will not be charged any interest. Strive to be one of "those" customers.
- If you borrow from an individual, be sure to repay the loan on time, as scheduled, just as you would with a credit card. You're building a reputation with each payment made, or each payment late or missed.

- Home equity loans can allow you to borrow money from yourself, using your home as collateral. Just be cautious. This is your home, your home base, that you are putting on the line in case you default on your loan.

BORROWING BEANS

Think of saving as buying and storing food in your pantry, where food is considered to be money. That enables you, when it's time for your next meal, to go to the pantry and pull out something to eat. If you have not stored anything in your pantry (if you have not *saved*), you cannot eat. What to do? You must go to your next-door neighbor and *borrow* some food. The understanding, though, is that for each can of food (let's say beans) you borrow, you must give him back an extra can of beans for each month that goes by before you repay him his can of beans. If you wait three months before returning him his can of beans, you now *owe* him four cans of beans—the one you borrowed, plus three more as *interest*. So you got to enjoy eating the one can of beans you borrowed from him, but had to repay him *that* can of beans, plus an *additional* three cans that you will never get to enjoy. Interest is like that. It is like having to give away cans of beans that you had to buy with your earnings but then didn't get to enjoy, use, or eat at all. You simply give it to someone else. They will then get to enjoy eating your

cans of beans. (Now you know one possible source for
the saying "That company ate my lunch!")

Debt-free

The ultimate goal that I encourage you to embrace is to become
debt-free. I realize that, for most people who have been in debt for
all of their adult life, this may seem like a dream. Wishful thinking,
you may say. But it is a possibility. Families and individuals
manage to accomplish it every day. Dave Ramsey, a well-known
financial management speaker and author, encourages those who
become debt-free to call in to his radio show. His callers are then
invited to yell out, "I'm debt-free!"

It does require self-discipline and living in harmony with
financial principles, but the results are worth it. The feeling that
comes from being debt-free, where you don't owe anyone anything,
is one of deep satisfaction and peace. You feel more in control of
your life than you've felt in a long time. Once you are debt-free,
you can begin to save more, invest more, and even be better able to
help others. As your savings and investments grow you're building a
bigger and better cushion against any financial emergency that may
come into your life. You begin to live in a new way, firmly in control
of your financial life.

In general, it is much better not to borrow. A key goal should be
to work to become debt-free. There are some occasions where
borrowing can be useful and wise, but they are limited. Borrowing

is often caused by discontent and lack of preparation. We want more than we have. We want more than we can afford. Therefore we borrow. In so doing, we allow someone else to make money off us. We enable *them* to live a successful financial life rather than *us*!

Chapter 15

Principle of Saving

"The quickest way to double your money is to fold it in half and put it in your back pocket."

—Will Rogers

PRINCIPLE 11:
Spend Less Than You Earn.

Although it may not seem so now, you will not always be able to work physically. You must take steps to set up your money so that it can work for you when you're no longer able to work for it. That requires saving money so that you can then invest it. If you set aside enough in regular savings throughout your working career, you will accumulate enough to make a difference later in your life by having a nest egg to draw on.

Recognize that when you're early in your lifetime of saving, the growth of your savings will be very slow. That is normal; it's just the way it is in those early years. The greatest annual growth in your savings will occur in the latest years of your career, when you have already accumulated a significant amount. The greater the amount of savings invested, the greater the amount of growth that happens each year. See the examples below for the annual growth at various levels of savings. Remember, as you are able to set aside increasingly larger amounts, the power of compounding begins to dramatically work in your favor. We will discuss compounding later in this chapter.

> 5% annual return on $ 1,000 = $ 50
>
> 5% annual return on $ 10,000 = $ 500
>
> 5% annual return on $ 100,000 = $ 5,000
>
> 5% annual return on $1,000,000 = $ 50,000

I know I discussed this already in the chapter on spending, but the next paragraph covers such an important point that I include it here as well. Spending and saving are inextricably linked, in that you cannot both save and spend a specific dollar. You must do one or the other. So it's appropriate to include these thoughts in both chapters.

In order to save, you must *adjust your lifestyle to match your income level.* In the early years of your working career, both your income and your savings will likely be very small and modest. You must diligently strive to live within your means at that point, not beyond your means. That will enable you to stay out of debt, steadily save, and gradually build up your assets.

This means that in order to save, you must live *below* your means! That may seem unrealistic to you, and something that no one could do. Fortunately, there are examples of families who *do* succeed in accomplishing this. I know an elderly couple with modest jobs who carefully saved not only in the early years of their marriage, but throughout their lives. For investments, they did not invest in high-return stocks or stock mutual funds; instead, they purchased low-interest CDs. Yet they were able to accumulate a nice six-figure retirement portfolio by living simply—and well below their means. I would wager that many of the successful middle-aged and older families you know that are now financially well-off went through many years of frugal living in the early years of their working careers.

A general rule of thumb is to aim to save 15 percent of what you earn. This is an amount that's doable, eventually, for most people, and results in a nice accumulation of funds over time. That may seem to be an impossible amount to save each month at this point. If you have to start with saving only a small amount, say $25 or $50 per month, do it. You must start somewhere. Then slowly but diligently increase the amount that you're saving. Utilize a pay raise as an opportunity to increase your monthly savings without affecting your take-home pay.

Short-Term vs. Long-Term Savings

You will need to accumulate savings for two purposes. First of all, you will need savings to cover short-term needs. There are at least three needs that you may wish to include. The first is to handle any unexpected emergencies, such as medical issues or major car or household repairs. The second is to accumulate funds for the future purchase of more expensive items, such as a car, major appliances, or vacation. The third is to provide funds to cover minimum required household expenses for at least three months in case you lose your job. These funds should all be kept in easily accessible accounts, such as savings and checking accounts.

How much to aim to have in short-term savings? A general recommendation is $1000-$2000 set aside to cover unexpected emergencies. Savings needed for future planned purchases depends on what your planned purchases may be. And finally, your monthly take home pay, tripled, will result in the amount needed in case of a disruption in your income.

The second purpose would be for long-term savings, which is often referred to as your retirement nest egg. This type of savings has years in which to grow and could be in accounts that may not be easily accessible. These long-term savings are often held in Individual Retirement Accounts (IRAs), 401(k)s, and other similar retirement-oriented accounts, which will be discussed in more detail in the next chapter on investing. (Note that the IRS calls an IRA an Individual Retirement *Arrangement*, but most other sources refer to it as Individual Retirement *Account*.)

Determining how much to save for retirement involves quite a few variables, and is beyond the scope of this book. For most people, saving 15% of your regular income for retirement is a commonly accepted way to aggressively save toward that goal.

Compound Interest

A word about the impact of compound interest is in order here. Compound interest can generally be defined as *earning interest on any interest that was earned in a previous period of time*. Let me illustrate. Let's pick large numbers to make it easier to see the impact. Let's assume that you invest $100,000 in a three-year CD that pays 5 percent interest, and the interest compounds monthly. That means that they calculate and pay interest every month. (Note that most CDs would only compound quarterly, but let's not fuss with that at this point.)

When you first deposit the $100,000, your balance is exactly that—$100,000. At the end of the first month, the bank calculates the interest to determine how much to pay you. Since they pay 5 percent per year, we divide that by 12 to determine the interest rate to apply each month. 5 percent, or .05, divided by 12 = 0.004167. So the interest earned in the first month is $100,000 x 0.004167, or $416.70.

The next month after that, in order to calculate the interest to be paid, they would not multiply times the original amount but by the *new balance*, which includes the interest paid the previous month as well. The interest earned is thus *compounded.* Our calculation would be $100,416.70 x 0.004167, or $418.40.

Included below (Table 1), you can see the growth of this CD over its three years.

Table 1

Month	Beginning Balance	Monthly Interest Rate	Interest Paid	Ending Balance	Accumulated Interest

Month	Beginning Balance	Monthly Interest Rate	Interest Paid	Ending Balance	Accumulated Interest
1	$100,000.00	0.004167	$416.70	$100,416.70	$416.70
2	$100,416.70	0.004167	$418.40	$100,835.10	$835.10
3	$100,835.10	0.004167	$420.15	$101,255.25	$1,255.25
4	$101,255.25	0.004167	$421.90	$101,677.15	$1,677.15
*	*	*	*	*	*
*	*	*	*	*	*
*	*	*	*	*	*
33	$114,231.47	0.004167	$475.96	$114,707.44	$14,707.44
34	$114,707.44	0.004167	$477.95	$115,185.38	$15,185.38
35	$115,185.38	0.004167	$479.94	$115,665.32	$15,665.32
36	$115,665.32	0.004167	$481.94	$116,147.26	$16,147.26

GROWTH OF A THREE-YEAR CD AT 5% WITH COMPOUNDING

Total interest earned $16,147.26

For comparison purposes, I have included on the next page (Table 2) the same three-year CD but *without* compounding, which is called *simple interest.* In this instance, it is as though the interest that's paid each month is simply set aside into a savings account, which pays no interest. In this example, removing compounding results in the CD earning $1,146.06 *less* over the three-year period.

Table 2

GROWTH OF A THREE-YEAR CD AT 5% **WITHOUT COMPOUNDING**					
Month	Beginning Balance	Monthly Interest Rate	Interest Paid	Ending Balance	Accumulated Interest
1	$100,000.00	0.004167	$416.70	$100,000.00	$416.70
2	$100,000.00	0.004167	$416.70	$100,000.00	$833.40
3	$100,000.00	0.004167	$416.70	$100,000.00	$1,250.10
4	$100,000.00	0.004167	$416.70	$100,000.00	$1,666.80
*	*	*	*	*	*
*	*	*	*	*	*
*	*	*	*	*	*
33	$100,000.00	0.004167	$416.70	$100,000.00	$13,751.10
34	$100,000.00	0.004167	$416.70	$100,000.00	$14,167.80
35	$100,000.00	0.004167	$416.70	$100,000.00	$14,584.50
36	$100,000.00	0.004167	$416.70	$100,000.00	$15,001.20

Total interest earned $15,001.20

Note that the difference between compounding and not compounding is greater the longer the timespan involved. If we were to continue with the example above, but extend it out to a thirty-year CD of $100,000, earning 5 percent, you would find the following when comparing the two:

Total interest earned on a thirty-year CD

with compounding	$346,774.58
without compounding	$150,012.00
Difference	$196,762.58

Compounding of interest basically means that the longer you can leave your money invested, and the larger the balance, the faster it will grow.

PENNY INTEREST

Think of the act of saving as similar to creating a large pile of pennies in a massive grain silo. When you first start, there are only a few coins rattling around in the bottom of the silo where you're storing them. But year after year, the pile begins to grow inside of the silo. Also, something special begins to happen. The pile of coins begins to slowly grow *even when you don't add any pennies to the pile!* It's beginning to grow on its own. (It is earning interest.) You notice that, as the pile gets *higher*, it also grows *faster*. (This is compound interest at work—earning interest on the interest from the previous months.)

Eventually, the pile reaches the top inside of the silo. But you notice that there is an overflow chute that leads from the top of the silo to the top of another silo next to it. This other silo, which also started out empty, is now beginning to fill just from the overflow from the first silo. This demonstrates the fact that your silo of pennies can potentially continue to grow, even as you are withdrawing pennies each month to live on. If you can just take out less each month than the amount that it grows during that time, then it will continue to stay full and continue to supply an overflowing amount that can be withdrawn through the overflow chute. That means you have saved enough to retire on, and you can continue to withdraw a sum of pennies each month. You can live off the pennies coming into the overflow silo in the form of interest earned, keeping the first silo perpetually full.

There is a difference between saving and hoarding. Saving is preparing prudently for the future. Hoarding is compulsively clinging to everything you have out of a fear of the future. Hoarding is never using; instead, you forever grip tightly. You probably won't be tempted to hoard your money and become miserly, but it has happened occasionally. It's always good to watch out for such tendencies in ourselves.

FIRE

There is currently a radical new savings trend called FIRE. This is an acronym for Financial Independence, Retire Early. With this approach, a (typically) young person will determine to live extremely simply, with their expenses cut to the bone. It is not uncommon for it to be a goal for a FIRE-adherent to live on 30 percent of their income and save 70 percent. This will rapidly accelerate the rate at which they accumulate savings, and they hope it will enable them to retire from active work at a very young age, say thirty-five to forty-five years old. I present this not as a serious option that I advocate, but as an example of what is possible by decreasing spending and increasing saving, albeit to an extreme degree. There is quite a bit available on the Internet about FIRE if this intrigues you and you wish to learn more. Who knows, you may decide to take the plunge and do this yourself!

In summary, saving is, by and large, simply resisting the urge to spend. It also reflects the understanding that, to attain wealth takes time and patience, not borrowing. You can't *borrow* your way to wealth; you must *save* your way to wealth. There are no shortcuts— no matter how convincing the casino and lottery ads may seem.

Chapter 16

Principle of Investing

*"If you don't find a way to make money while you sleep,
you will work until you die."*

—Warren Buffett

PRINCIPLE 12:
Investing Is Making Your Money
Work for You.

S aving is determining how much to set aside rather than spend, then doing so. *Investing* is deciding where to put the money that you have saved. Investing is a broad topic, and reams of information about it are available in other publications, many of them devoted exclusively to investing. For the purposes of this book, a few basic tenets are discussed with the intent of clarifying some misunderstandings regarding investing. My goal is also to encourage you to explore investing, perhaps more than you have before. It is a great way to grow your wealth.

The term "investing" may conjure up the image of a wealthy Wall Street stock broker, perhaps wearing an expensive silk suit, having achieved multiple academic degrees and certifications in finance. If you have this perspective, then investing may seem to be difficult, tedious, and fraught with the risk of making bad decisions. While it is true that stock brokers on Wall Street do, in fact, make investments, it is also true that *each of us make investments daily*. Let's step back and look at investing from a broader perspective for a minute.

You could say that investing is simply choosing where and how to use your assets. You may feel that you don't have any assets to invest; therefore the topic doesn't apply to you. Actually, each of us possesses quite a variety of assets. We all get twenty-four hours of *time* each day, for example. We all have a reservoir of *energy* to be used. We all have *knowledge* about many things that can be used in various ways. And we all possess some *financial assets*, however meager, even if only a bank account or physical cash.

Let's take a look at the asset of time as an example. Here are some ways we may invest our time.

- Daily working at a job—earning a living
- Initiating and maintaining relationships—spending time with others
- Acquiring and maintaining possessions—homes, cars, boats, appliances, etc.
- Maintaining our emotional health—hobbies, travel, and entertainment
- Maintaining our mind and intellect—reading, studying, thinking, and writing
- Maintaining our body—exercise, sleep, and diet
- Planning for and maintaining our financial assets— saving and investing

All of these require us to *invest* our time in them in order to accomplish them, do they not?

We are all, thus, investors. We choose to invest our time, energy, attention, and money into various things every day. It's also true that we expect to get a *return* for our investment in each of these things. If you invest in a new car, you expect to not only receive a return of having reliable transportation, but also a more intangible return of the pleasure of looking at it, driving it, and utilizing any new and desirable features that it possesses. If we're disappointed in any of those areas, it may be said that we did not get a good return on our investment.

The term "investing" usually carries with it the implication that a conscious decision has been made regarding the investment. I would propose that we all do, indeed, invest ourselves in things, but we may or may not give much thought to the decision. In general, though, if we do think about it and make it a conscious decision, the outcome will usually be better. We are more likely to get a good return on our investment, no matter what type it may be. If we don't give it much thought, then we can end up spending our time, energy, and money on things that we really don't value highly.

The goal is to invest wisely and get the best return for your investment. We have been discussing the assets of time, energy, and so forth. Let's now turn to the topic of investing our *financial* assets. You are an investor, so you might as well be a good investor. Let's see how you can get a good return on your financial assets, as well as your time.

The first point is brief but basic. As was mentioned earlier, you must save before you can invest. If you don't *have* any financial assets, you certainly can't invest them. So first things first, remember that you must exercise the discipline of saving, then you can begin to select where to invest those savings, those assets. (I recognize that you may have inherited financial assets, or received them as a gift or prize, but for most of us, we must simply accumulate financial assets by saving from our income.)

Observe that investing your money is making your money work for you, rather than you working for your money. Just as when you put in a day's work and receive a day's wages or salary, so an investment puts in a day's worth of earning interest for you (or a day's worth of capital gains—more on that later). The more money that you have invested, the greater the interest it will earn. Eventually, you may get to the point where the interest you're earning, and the capital gains growth your investments yield each month, exceeds the amount you're earning from your employment. At that point, you will have the option of quitting your job and living off your investments. *(See Penny Interest in chapter 15.)*

Now that you have some savings set aside, where to invest it? For our purposes, I have separated financial investments into four basic categories and included some examples of each. There are other ways of grouping investments, as well as many potential subgroups, but for our purposes, these four will provide a general framework of where you can choose to invest.

1) Physical Asset Investments

The first category of investment is physical assets. This can include anything tangible and physical. Our homes, for example, are a significant physical asset. Other personal property, such as autos, furniture, computers, appliances, tools, and so on, are all examples of physical assets. Most assets of this type depreciate, or go down in value, over time, with real estate being the most notable exception. For that reason, they are not usually considered a way to grow your overall wealth; instead, they are something that simply provides a useful function to you. You might feel that buying physical assets is not really investing, but the point to note is that when you buy a physical asset, you have chosen, by default, *not* to invest in something else. You are using, or investing, your money in these items rather than in another type of investment, such as a bank CD or stocks. As was mentioned earlier, you can't both spend and save (or invest) the same dollar.

There are a few physical assets that do have the potential to grow in value over time. Real estate is probably the best example of this. It is unique in that there is an obvious limit on the available supply. As is often noted, "They aren't making any more of it." Much has been written about investing in real estate, and if that appeals to you, then I encourage you to explore that further.

Another type of physical asset that can appreciate in value would be collectibles, such as coins, stamps, antique cars, art and other items. A collection can provide emotional satisfaction to the hobbyist, but it also may have the potential to grow in value over time. The challenge for the collector is to predict which collectibles will increase in value, and which will not.

One more type of physical asset that's sometimes viewed as a potential growth investment is gold or silver. This would typically be in the form of bullion, which is a coin or bar that's minted and sold simply as a standardized way of measuring it. A silver eagle $1 bullion coin, for example, has very little value as a collectible coin. Its value is that it is guaranteed by the US mint to contain exactly one ounce of 99.9 percent pure silver. The person who invests in bullion is hoping that physical gold or silver will, over time, increase in value.

2) Cash Investments

The second category is cash and cash-like investments. This includes the physical currency that you have in your wallet or purse, and also the funds that you have in a bank savings or checking account. These are considered cash-like because banks pay very little interest on them so they are essentially a place to store your cash. You invest in them because of the ready access they offer you and the security of your funds being insured up to $250,000 against loss by the FDIC (Federal Deposit Insurance Corporation). Even in the case of a bank going bankrupt, which is extremely rare, your funds are guaranteed by the FDIC. A checking account also might offer various other benefits, such as check-writing privileges, overdraft protection, and the flexibility of a debit card.

Cash is an investment that does not grow much, if at all. Banks typically offer only a tiny rate of interest, likely not even enough to keep up with the rate of inflation. The principal advantages of cash and cash-like investments is that they are insured (if they are in a bank) and are readily available.

3) Debt Investments

The third category is a broad group that can be labeled debt investments. With them, you are, in effect, "loaning" your money to a bank or individual with agreed-upon terms of repayment. In essence, they owe you a "debt" that they must repay with interest. Examples of this are bank CDs, savings bonds, municipal bonds, bond mutual funds, and personal loans that you make to family members or friends. You could even call a bond almost the same thing as a loan, since that's the function it performs. The return on these will usually be better than the return on cash and cash-like investments, but not as good as with equity investments.

The primary difference between a CD or bond and a savings account is that you agree not to get your money back for a specified period of time. A CD, for example, will typically be issued for a specific timespan, such as one, two, or three years. If you choose to ask for your money back sooner than the full term of the CD, then you agree to pay a penalty in the form of reduced interest, which is spelled out clearly in the CD prospectus.

4) Equity Investments

The fourth and final category is an equity investment, which is different than the others discussed previously. With this you are not buying a depreciating physical asset such as an auto. You are not parking cash with a bank. You are not making a debt investment in a CD or bond. With equity investing, you buy a *share* of the ownership in an asset. The asset could be a home, where the percentage of the home that you own is stated as your "equity" in the home. In this way, buying any real estate can be a form of equity investment in that you are building equity, or ownership, as you pay off the loan taken out to purchase the real estate. Another common asset to own is a share in a publicly traded company. This is typically in the form of shares invested in a stock mutual fund, a stock Exchange Traded Fund (ETF), or an individual stock.

Buying equity in a company allows you the opportunity to participate in the creative, exciting, innovative labor of others. You may not have the education or skillset to work at Microsoft, for example, but by investing in the company of Microsoft through buying some of its stock, you share in the growth and prosperity of that company. The success of Microsoft, or of any company, is directly related to the effectiveness of the staff and management in executing all of the tasks associated with that business. All of the things that go into running a company—picking the products or services they will sell, selecting a target market, hiring and training staff, managing costs, developing innovative and lucrative solutions to real problems—are all done by people. As an investor, you get to "piggyback," sharing in the success of this cadre of talented, hard-working professionals without ever having to work for even a minute for the company as their employee. What a wonderful privilege and opportunity!

In addition to paying out a portion of profits in the form of dividends, your stock equity has the potential to grow in value through stock share price appreciation. This simply means that as more buyers are interested in a particular stock, the price per share of that stock gradually goes up. It's basically an example of the law of supply and demand. Think of it like attending an estate sale auction, where the price of a used, collectible tractor may go up and up if there are several buyers interested in purchasing it. Thus, the demand is increasing but the supply is not—there's only one tractor being auctioned. Over longer spans of time (years, for example), the share price of some stocks can rise quite dramatically. Amazon, for example, could be purchased for $1.54 per share in June 1997, but as of February 15, 2022, a share was worth $3130.21. Now that is what you call an increase in the value of your asset!

You also have the option of selling your stock equity investment any time the markets are open, which is generally Monday through Friday year-round. This ability to easily sell your assets and thus convert them to cash is considered *liquidity*. If something is harder to quickly convert to cash, such as real estate, then it is considered *illiquid*, or not liquid.

BILL'S AUTO REPAIR SHOP: A STORY ABOUT EQUITY VS. DEBT INVESTING

As an illustration of the difference between buying a bond or CD and buying a share of stock, let's consider a hypothetical friend of yours named Bill, who is planning to buy an auto repair shop. If you extend a loan to him to pay for the shop, that could be considered equivalent to buying a bond that he made available for purchase. He agrees to pay you a set percentage of interest and, perhaps, repay a specific amount each month, with the entire amount to be repaid by an agreed-upon future date.

Now, in contrast to that, let's say that he instead decides to raise money to buy the shop by selling shares in his business. He issues $100,000 in stock in the form of 100 *shares* of stock, each costing $1000. You like your friend, and you think he is going to be successful, so you decide to buy twenty shares of his stock for $20,000. You are now a 20 percent owner of his company. If his company makes a profit, then he can pay you a *dividend*, or a percentage of the profits, based on how many shares you own. Dividends are usually paid quarterly. If he decides to pay $100 dividend per share, then your dividend would be calculated as $100 x 20 shares = $2000. (Note that, strictly speaking, paying dividends is not dependent upon earning profits, but let's not worry about that at this point.)

Now let's say that over time, he runs the business wisely, expands, and with his profits buys three more repair shops. The shares are now viewed as more desirable by others who would like to own a share of the company.

For purposes of the illustration, assume there is a market where the shares of his company can be bought and sold. If someone is now willing to pay you $1500 per share for your stock, then your stock has *appreciated* by 50 percent, since it has gone up in value from $1000 per share to $1500 per share. You decide that you're ready to take your money out of the business, so you elect to sell all twenty of your shares at $1500 each, for a total of $30,000. You have just made $10,000 on your original $20,000 investment. Your increase in value is called a *capital gain*. A business is considered to be capital, and your value per share went up, or "gained" in value.

There is an associated risk with investing in stocks though. There is the possibility that Bill does not do a successful job of running his shop. Perhaps his customer-relations skills are not good. Perhaps he specialized in foreign cars, and there are not enough of them in his city that need repair work done. There are any number of reasons why a business might fail. If he decides he must go out of business, then he will sell it for what he can get. If it is $50,000, then he will distribute that amount to the holders of the 100 shares of stock, and each share will get back $500. Your twenty shares are now only worth 20 x $500 = $10,000. You have lost $10,000 on your original $20,000 investment. Your decrease in value is called a capital loss.

Advantages of Equity Investing

In general, over the past forty to sixty years, the US stock market, in the form of the S&P 500 Index, has returned an average of 7–10 percent per year. That may not sound like much, but it is typically higher than what is commonly paid out in interest on bank savings accounts or even bonds. This is the primary reason to consider investing in equities—they have the potential to have a far greater return than other investments. (This growth potential is also true for investing in real estate, which can be considered a type of equity investment because it involves ownership of the asset.)

The US stock markets have been one of the greatest generators of wealth in the world. I am a firm believer in the value of everyone participating in the opportunity that the stock markets present. I do recognize that there are risks associated with it, and that an investor needs to be prudent and educated about the investments he or she is choosing. You can be thoughtless and reckless in your investments in the stock markets just as in anything else. The markets are not magic. They are simply an opportunity for you to participate, financially, in the economic engines of the world—the companies which provide all of the products and services we need and want.

Some Basic Strategies for Investing in Stock Equities

Optimistic Mindset

You must deliberately work to have the right mindset about investing. This is critical to your financial success.

- If you think investing is complicated, risky, and that you will never learn how to do it, then you never will. What if you thought that way about driving an automobile? You would never have learned to drive a car. It helps that you grew up riding in cars and gaining familiarity as a result. Exposure to stocks and the stock market can help in the same way.
- You must seek to cultivate an optimistic "can do" attitude—"I can learn this!"

Manage Your Expectations

You must manage your expectations with stock investments. Realize that stocks are different in that their value can go up or down, while a debt instrument, like a bond, will grow slowly but steadily up in value. Cash, of course, will maintain its value and may grow slightly, but your cash balance does not go down. With an equity investment, you must look at the long-term *trend* of the stock price, not the day-to-day swings up or down in the share price. You must have a longer-term perspective.

Be Your Own Investment Manager

I encourage you to take a shot at being your own investment manager. It's a little more involved than opening a bank savings account, but it can be learned. You will need to make use of basic computer skills, so if your skills are rusty or you're unfamiliar with computers, I suggest taking a class at your local community college to get up to speed in that area.

If you're not comfortable being your own investment manager, then another option would be to contact a broker in your local community and discuss setting up an investment account. Most will do a good job of managing your investments, but they will charge you for that service. That is how they make their income; they are simply receiving pay for a service they provide. If you manage your investments yourself using an online brokerage, there will be no cost to buy or sell a stock. There will be some charges if you choose to invest in mutual funds, but you will still avoid the overall broker fee.

Open an Account with an Online Brokerage

If you're ready to try investing in stocks and managing them yourself, the first step is to open an account at an online brokerage. There are several good firms to choose from, such as Schwab, TD Ameritrade, E*Trade, Robinhood, and others. I personally have used Schwab for many years and like their service.

Start Small

As a strategy, I recommend that you start small in your investing. Your first purchase may simply be one share of stock in a company that you like and respect. I suggest starting by investing no more than $500 or $1000, spread out by buying shares in several companies. Then you can begin to observe how they go up or down each day and see how they compare to the rest of the market. Each investment, no matter how small, is progress toward your goal of becoming a knowledgeable, successful investor.

Manage Risk

I have a chapter devoted to the topic of risk earlier in the book, but let's briefly review risk here again as it relates to your financial investments. The goal is for your investments to go up in value. Conversely, you want to minimize the risk that your investments will go down in value. I have noted below some suggested ways to manage your risk.

- Don't put all your eggs in one basket. Money you will need for monthly spending, for emergencies, and for planned major purchases should be in bank savings accounts, checking accounts, or CDs. That's one basket. Your house, vehicles, furniture, and all of your physical assets is another basket. Your stock investments thus become a third basket, and it can have two components. One might be more conservative index mutual funds or ETFs, and the second would be individual stocks. Have a good base of the more conservative funds first, then slowly add individual stocks.
- Avoid companies that are doing poorly.
- Diversify—buy stocks that are in a variety of industries. Buy a mix of small, medium, and large companies.
- Avoid a short-term mindset, which can lead you to panic or to excitedly splurge on a stock that seems like a "sure thing."
- Avoid stock investing products that you don't understand. Most are not suitable for the beginning investor. I recommend you avoid these until you have learned more.

Invest in What You Know

We all are familiar with many products and services. If you have a company that you particularly like, whether it's Amazon, Walmart, or Best Buy, do some research on their stock. I suggest that you start with one or two of them as the first stocks that you buy. Many companies do very well financially and can provide a nice investment base. If you don't have any idea what a company does or sells, I don't recommend investing in it, no matter how much someone else says it's a great buy. I *do* recommend that you begin regularly watching that stock's share price to see how it's doing, and that you begin learning about it. Then, after you have learned enough, you may feel comfortable investing in it. You don't need to become a specialist in that company, just understand enough of what they do to be able to judge whether you think it will be a good investment or not.

Keep Learning

The world is continually changing. The investment world is no different. I invite you to set aside time each week to read up on investing and on any particular companies you might be interested in. There is an abundance of free information available at your fingertips on the Internet. By using the Google search engine and spending a little time, you can find out a lot. Keep on learning and growing. That's part of the fun.

Summary of Investing in Stock Equities

- You are an owner, not a loaner.
- Share prices can go up or down (sometimes dramatically) every day.
- Investing in stocks requires a long-term perspective.
- You receive dividends per share, not interest.

- You will have capital gains and losses.
- Diversification becomes important (generally not as much of an issue for a debt investment).
- Stock investing involves more risk but offers greater potential long-term return.
- Choosing what companies to invest in requires some study and prudence.
- Is it gambling? Not unless you don't apply yourself to learning how and what to invest.

Consider Tax-deferred Assets

In order to encourage participation in retirement accounts, Congress has established two general types of retirement accounts that offer significant tax advantages, the IRA (Individual Retirement Account) and the 401(k). (There are other retirement programs available, but these two are the most common and prominent. Any other tax-deferred savings plans would work similarly.) If you have already invested in either or both of these, you are on the right track. If you have not, I invite you to consider doing so. Let's look briefly at each of them.

The IRA, or Individual Retirement Account, allows you to defer paying taxes on up to $6,000 per year (for 2022) for an individual when you invest it in an IRA. You will not pay taxes on those funds until you begin to withdraw them in retirement. (The maximum amount you can invest per year changes periodically, as Congress updates the law.)

The Roth IRA works similarly, except you still pay taxes on the amount you invest in your Roth IRA, but then you don't have to pay any tax when you withdraw it in retirement. You also don't pay tax on any *increase in value* due to earned interest or capital appreciation. That is a significant benefit!

A 401(k) is similar to an IRA, except it is administered by an employer and only offered to its employees. Some companies also offer a Roth 401(k) as an option, and it works very similar to the Roth IRA. One nice advantage of either type of 401(k) is that companies will often contribute to an employee's 401(k) account, usually in the form of a partial match. For example, they may contribute 50 percent of what an employee contributes up to a stated maximum. A common match would be to contribute 50 percent of an employee's contribution until the employee's contribution hits 6 percent of their wages for that pay period. If the employee contributes $60, the company would contribute $30. That is essentially free money from the company, which you forgo if you don't contribute up to the maximum amount that they match. A second advantage of the 401(k) is that the contribution limits are much higher. An individual can contribute up to $20,500 per year (for 2022) into their 401(k) account, which is higher than the maximum of $6,000 permitted with an IRA.

There are various other specific guidelines for both IRAs and 401(k)s. The bank or broker that you work with can help you understand all of the options or, in the case of a 401(k), your employer would be your resource to consult. There is also excellent information available on the Internet about both IRAs and 401(k)s. I strongly recommend that you check out both of these investment options and consider including them as part of your overall investment plan.

Investing is learning about the many ways you can put your money to work, then choosing from among those options the ones that seem to line up with your personal values, your comfort level with risk, and your ambitions. It is important what you choose to invest in. It makes a difference. Just leaving your funds in checking and savings accounts will ensure that you don't lose them, but you will sacrifice all of the potential gain you could have had if you had invested in bonds or equities.

Chapter 17

Principle of Giving

"How selfish soever man may be supposed, there are evidently some principles in his nature, which interest him in the fortune of others, and render their happiness necessary to him, though he derives nothing from it, except the pleasure of seeing it".

—Adam Smith

PRINCIPLE 13:
Giving Benefits Both the Giver and
the Receiver of the Gift.

A s you become successful in managing your financial life, your assets will grow. One of the greatest privileges that comes with increased wealth is the opportunity to help or to bless others. It is not a requirement, of course, but an opportunity. In order for your wealth to be something you control, rather than having it control you, you must be willing to be generous. If you become miserly, hanging on to every penny so that you maximize your wealth, you will find yourself unsatisfied with what you have.

If, on the other hand, you hold your wealth with a loose hand rather than a tight grip, you will find it both enjoyable and rewarding to share your wealth with others. You will feel good about yourself and about the good you're doing in the world. One word that effectively defines this manner of living is *altruism*.

"Altruism is the unselfish concern for other people— doing things simply out of a desire to help, not because you feel obligated to out of duty, loyalty, or religious reasons. It involves acting out of concern for the well-being of other people. In some cases, these acts of altruism lead people to jeopardize themselves to help others. Such behaviors are often performed unselfishly and without any expectations of reward. Other instances, known as reciprocal altruism, involve taking actions to help others with the expectation that they will offer help in return. Everyday life is filled with small acts of altruism, from holding the door for strangers to giving money to people in need. News stories often focus on grander cases of altruism, such as a man who dives into an icy river to rescue a drowning stranger or a donor who gives thousands of dollars to a local charity."[15]

In an earlier chapter we discussed the psychology of money and how it can affect us in many ways. The effect of hoarding your wealth is that your mind and your thoughts will be primarily focused on *yourself*. Your attention will be directed toward growing your wealth further. This persistent focus on yourself can become a corrosive influence in your life. Specifically, your relationship with others may deteriorate. People will eventually figure out your motivation and objectives and will be repelled by your self-centeredness. You may find others ingratiating themselves with you, but it will more than likely be so that they can receive some financial gain from you. They like you for your money and for what you can do for them. Not a great basis for building a friendship or even just a mutually beneficial relationship.

On the other hand, if you're generous with your wealth, then you will find that your focus is on *others* rather than yourself. You will look for opportunities to make a positive difference in the life of those you encounter as you go about your day. There are many people who, for various reasons, have had a rough time in life financially. They may have worked hard and tried to be both prudent and wise, but circumstances have worked against them for one reason or another. With a financial boost at the right time, you can make a dramatic difference in the life of someone who is struggling in this way, helping them to get over a hump of discouragement that may have them stymied and disheartened. In doing so, you will feel pleased that you were able to make a difference in the life of another.

Note that this does not mean you simply shower others with money; it means you exercise good judgment on how to most effectively help someone financially. It often is *not* the best thing to simply give money to someone. You must decide how much to give and in what form. Perhaps you want to encourage a young person early in their career to focus on saving, and you give them some funds to put into an IRA or a Roth IRA. A single mother may need the gift of an airline ticket so she can visit her ailing parents in another state or country. There are many wonderful charities and church organizations in the world that provide help, education, and encouragement to others. Their mission is to make the world a better place. You can choose to partner with one or several of those to help them accomplish that mission. The list of good charities is endless, but you get to decide the specific ones that appeal to you and which ones you will support.

We all want to feel that there is a purpose to our lives, that we make a difference. Whether we think about it much or not, we will each leave a legacy when we're gone. Those we have touched with our kindness and generosity will be forever changed, and grateful, that we were in their lives. But remember that you will be enriched as much, or perhaps more, than they will be. Giving is good for your soul. I encourage you to embrace giving as a crucially important component in successfully managing your personal financial life.

We accumulate money in order to make our lives more secure, comfortable, and enjoyable. Our goal is to live a rich, full, and happy life. True happiness and contentment, though, doesn't come simply from acquiring possessions; it comes from relationships. Giving provides us an opportunity to foster and deepen our connection to others in a way that enriches both them and us.

Principles About Trust

To be successful in your financial life, you will need to interact successfully with others. One crucial component in accomplishing that is trust. In order to trust an individual, group, or company, you have to believe three things about them. First, you must believe that they are honest, a person or company of *character*, who won't try to cheat or lie. Second, you must believe they are *competent*—capable of doing what they say they will do. Finally, you must believe they are *committed*—determined to do what they said they would do, regardless of any obstacles that might arise.

These next five chapters will deal with trust. We will first look at the unavoidable issue of dishonesty. Next, we will examine the key components of trust, including character, competency, and commitment and how influential each one is. We will finish by challenging you to be trustworthy yourself.

Chapter 18

Principle of Dishonesty

"Credibility and dishonesty are polar opposites, not just in motion, but also in motive. Credibility is driven by a selfless spirit of mutual respect. Dishonesty is driven by a selfish spirit of self-preservation."

—Jeremy Gove

PRINCIPLE 14:
There Will Always Be Dishonest People After Your Money.

"2020 was a tough year. Between the pandemic and the economic crisis, we all had our hands full. And scammers didn't take any time off either—2020 was a busy year for fraud. In 2020, the FTC got more than 2.2 million reports about fraud, with people telling us they lost nearly $3.3 billion."[16]

It is unfortunate, but each of us must guard against losing our money to dishonest businesses and individuals. Not everyone is ethical and honest in their dealings with others. Some seem to believe that if you allow yourself to be fooled by them, then it's your problem, not theirs. They appear to lack a moral compass and will do whatever it takes to make a buck.

Let me hasten to add that, thankfully, most people are not like that. The world would be a very dangerous and dysfunctional place if everyone had that approach to life! No, I believe that most people just want to live their lives in an honest and productive manner. We do need to realize, though, that there are those who would be happy to separate us from our hard-earned dollars by any means possible. To be forewarned is to be forearmed.

How do we guard against others taking advantage of us? The best way is to learn some of the most common ways that dishonest people try to accomplish that. There are two broad categories of dishonesty that you will encounter. Let's examine both of them, then touch briefly on ethical marketing. We will finish with some tips on recognizing and avoiding dishonest offerings.

Criminal Dishonesty

The first dishonesty is criminal, where you pay money for something that you do not receive. If someone is caught doing this type of activity, they can be arrested, prosecuted, and punished to the full extent of the law.

An example of this would be an email purporting to be from a government agent in Nigeria, who states that they need to distribute $5 million from an estate, and they want your help to accomplish that. They purport to offer to give you a lot of money from this "estate." All you have to do is send them some money first, perhaps a few hundred dollars, so they can process the paperwork. Of course, after you send the funds, you will never receive any of this supposed wealth.

Another example would be the grandparent scam. My father fell for this one when someone called posing as one of Dad's grandsons and claiming that he was in trouble. He was in jail, he said, not because of anything he had done, but because he was a passenger in a car that had been stopped by the police, and the driver was intoxicated. As a result, all of those in the car were arrested. He was too embarrassed to call his dad, he said, so he was calling to ask "Grandpa" if he would send him $1500 to get him out of jail. The caller was very clever and seemed to know some things about my nephew that convinced my dad he was, indeed, his grandson. As many loving grandparents would do, my dad sent him the money, carefully following the detailed instructions he was given about how to do that. Fortunately, the next day my dad called his grandson to ask how he was doing. That triggered an effort to stop the payments, resulting in a loss of only $1000.

The best way to deal with scams, or other criminal offers, is to avoid them completely. As soon as you're presented with an offer like this, either from an email, letter, or phone call, an immediate red flag should pop up in the back of your mind. That's self-preservation at work, so let it do its job. The best way to avoid getting bitten by a snake is to move completely away from one as soon as you see it. Don't mess with it at all.

Criminal dishonesty examples:

- Identity theft
- Scams
- Fraudulent advertising
- "Get rich quick" schemes

Unethical Dishonesty

The second type of dishonesty is unethical but not criminal. This most often occurs when you're lured into buying something that you don't really want or need but are manipulated into purchasing it because of the salesperson's skill and tactics. In this case, you do actually receive something for your money, but you later realize that either the price was greatly inflated or the product doesn't give you the service you expected. Some would say this is just good salesmanship and that there isn't anything wrong with it. I say there is a very fine line between good, honest salesmanship and being unethical. Some of them would bristle at the suggestion that they are being dishonest, and perhaps rightfully so. But I would rather you be alert to their strategies and hopefully be able to make better decisions as a result.

Unethical dishonesty examples:
- Bait and switch
- Misleading advertising
- Fake reviews
- High-pressure sales

Ethical Selling and Marketing

There is a place for good salesmanship. There are thousands of people earning an honest living selling products or services to others. Zig Ziglar is an example of a very effective salesman who eventually became famous because of his skill. He wrote several books and developed into a highly sought-after public speaker. I am not trying to speak disparagingly of the sales industry as a whole, only of those who use underhanded and unethical tactics.

Ethical examples:
- Pointing out all the good features of a product
- Sharing how others missed out on an opportunity by hesitating
- Special, limited time offers
- Skillfully uncovering what the customer really wants and needs

Final Tips for Avoiding Dishonest Offerings

- Don't be greedy. Scams appeal to the base side of human nature by letting you think you will be getting something for nothing.
- Remember: if it seems too good to be true, it probably is.

- Keep your guard up. Remember that old adage, "A fool and his money are soon parted."

- If you encounter a scam, report it. "We can only fight scammers with your help. When you report to the FTC, your report is instantly available to more than 3,000 federal, state, and local law enforcers across the country who are looking to fight fraud. If you've spotted a scam, tell us at ReportFraud.ftc.gov."[17]

- Realize that scammers are resourceful and intelligent. They will continually be looking for new tactics to try.

- Social media was a great way to connect with friends while the pandemic had you keeping your distance. But reports to FTC's Consumer Sentinel Network suggest that social media websites and apps have become popular hangouts for scammers too. Reports that people lost money to scams that started on social media more than tripled in the past year, with a sharp increase in the second quarter of 2020.

- Reports about scams that started on social media have been increasing for years. In 2019, total reported losses to these frauds reached $134 million. But reported losses reached record highs, climbing to nearly $117 million in just the first six months of 2020. In that time, the reported scams that started on social media often related to online shopping, romance scams, and supposed economic relief or income opportunities.[18]

The world is a mixture of good and bad. It is not my goal to lead you to fear and worry over encountering dishonest people. But I do want you to consider that there are those who are attempting to separate you from your money by dishonesty, trickery, or underhanded means. You don't need to dwell on it or let it rob you of your inner peace, but you do need to be aware of it so that you can successfully defend against it.

Chapter 19

Principle of Character

*"I am not bound to win, but I am bound to be true.
I am not bound to succeed, but I am bound to live
up to what light I have."*

—Abraham Lincoln

PRINCIPLE 15:
Honesty Is the Mortar That Binds Together the Building Blocks of Success.

You have to be careful that you don't go overboard in your caution about the potential for others to be dishonest. If you do, you may become jaded and critical, suspicious of every action that anyone takes. That's not only a sad way to live, but a very unproductive one as well. You simply have to trust *some* people (many people, really) in order to be a successful member of society. Trust and honesty are what enables businesses and organizations to thrive. It is crucial.

Honesty is a good thing! It doesn't always get the billing it deserves these days. Our culture can sometimes give the impression that what is important is making sure you get ahead without worrying about the other guy. Not true! Honesty and character have much broader benefits and implications than you might realize.

- It allows an employee to confidently work for his employer because he trusts that they will pay him like they said they would.
- It enables a company to make plans that rely on, or trust, that employees will accomplish the tasks they have been assigned.
- It allows groups to work together productively.
- It allows families to function at their best, caring for one another.

- It allows a company to build a loyal following among their customers.
- It enables entrepreneurs to take bold steps in advancing their enterprise because they trust that the people working for them will give their best effort in trying to accomplish these steps.
- It enables leaders to be effective. People don't want to follow someone who is dishonest, even if only in little things.

Realize that it's probably better to be a little *too* trusting than too guarded. If you live your life full of suspicion, doubt, and distrust of others, that's a cold, lonely way to live. You always run the risk that you may be hurt when you trust, but to never trust anyone robs you of the opportunity to experience the delight of working with someone in a trusting relationship.

Trust is demonstrating your belief in the *character* of someone, believing they are honest and can be relied upon. That can be a great source of inspiration and encouragement to them. They won't want to let you down or disappoint you.

I do suggest you give your trust out in degrees though. If a small, initial trust proves to be warranted, then you can slowly give a little more. Don't give someone unknown a high degree of trust right at the outset. That can be risky.

Seek to find the right balance between giving and withholding trust. Don't be gullible or naive, but don't become cynical and unable to trust anyone either. Those are the two extremes you want to avoid. You want to be somewhere in the middle—willing to trust others but only when it is warranted.

Exemplifying trust, honesty, and character is a required part of becoming financially successful. It's what bonds people together in successful, lifelong partnerships, friendships, and even marriages. I encourage you to always keep honesty as a priority in your dealings with others.

Chapter 20

Principle of Competence

"I am, as I've said, merely competent. But in an age of incompetence, that makes me extraordinary."

—Billy Joel

PRINCIPLE 16:
Knowledge and Skill Determine Competence, Not Good Intentions.

This principle deals with another aspect of trust—competence. When you say that you trust someone, what does that mean? First of all, it means you feel they are honest—they won't try to cheat, steal, or lie. They have character. But it also means you believe they are *capable* of doing what they say they will do, that they are *competent*.

To receive the trust of someone you must have the skill, knowledge, strength, energy, and time to do what you say you will do. You must be *capable* of doing it.

This can take many forms. For example, someone may agree to meet you at a specific date and time to discuss a topic of mutual interest. If you trust them to do that, it means you believe they are competent to enter that planned date and time in their personal calendar, or use some other means, in order to remind them of their commitment to meet with you. Note that this competency doesn't have anything to do with honesty. They may have every intention of meeting with you, but if they are incompetent at managing their own schedule, then you may have doubts about whether they will remember to meet you. You doubt whether they are *competent* to record that commitment to you in such a way that it will remind them to actually follow through and meet with you.

I have observed that some people seem to feel if they honestly *intend* to remember an appointment, and honestly *intend* to be there on time, then that is all that counts—their intention. If they forget and don't show up, well, that's just part of life. They can't be expected to remember everything, right?

Continuing with this example, what occurs in your mind when someone fails to show up after they had committed to do so? You must assume that either something completely unexpected and important came up, or else they were not competent enough to use their personal calendar to remind them to meet with you. You may excuse this forgetfulness once or twice, but after that, you will begin to be very skeptical that they will show up unless you call and remind them to do so. You will have lost trust in them.

This belief in competency can be seen in other ways. Say your car is not running well, and you're considering taking it to a garage to get it checked out. If you have a friend who offers to fix it for you, you may decide to trust them to work on it. Your trust is not only based on whether they will show up as planned, but whether they are *competent* to diagnose and repair your car. If you don't think they are capable of doing so, then you won't entrust them to do it. You will make a polite comment, thanking them for the offer, but tell them you will take it to your regular garage instead.

Occasionally, you may ask someone to do a task when you know they may not *currently* have the knowledge or skill to do it. But if they commit to getting it done and you entrust them to do so, it means that you trust them to do *whatever it takes* to learn how to do it so that they *will* get it done. In this case, you are not trusting that they are already competent, but rather that they will get themselves competent enough to do it. You are actually trusting in their spirit of commitment to you, which we will talk about in the next chapter.

A person or company may honestly believe that they can do something. They think they can deliver a product or service in the manner they advertise they can. But the true test is whether they actually do it or not, no matter what they may profess or believe. Are they capable of getting it done? Does it happen as planned, or do they make an excuse instead?

Chapter 21

Principle of Commitment

*"Whenever you are asked if you can
do a job, tell 'em, 'Certainly I can!'
Then get busy and find out how to do it."*

—Theodore Roosevelt

PRINCIPLE 17:
A Promise Without Commitment Is a Fragile Hope Coated with Good Intentions.

Y ou can be quite capable of doing something you said in good faith that you would do. That doesn't mean you're going to get it done. It just means that you *could* get it done if you spent sufficient time on it and gave your energy and attention to doing it. There will always be little roadblocks thrown your way as you endeavor to accomplish something. When those show up, that's when your spirit of *commitment* will be revealed. Commitment is where the "rubber meets the road," as the saying goes. This is where you demonstrate what you're made of. Do you wilt at the first sign of trouble, or do you persevere?

Commitment implies that unless you are sick or injured, you will do whatever it takes to get the job done, short of breaking the law. You will not let problems or challenges stop you or deter you. That is the essence of what you look for in someone when you're trying to decide whether you can trust them or not, and that's what others will look for in you as well.

Commitment is not really needed until accomplishing something starts to become challenging or difficult. If getting something done is easy, no strong sense of commitment is really necessary or important. So unless you have been tested in this way, you don't really know how committed you are.

Some people seem to have a weak sense of commitment. Perhaps they have never really seen the need to truly commit to something. Others have always excused them if they failed to deliver, so they think, *Why worry about it now?*

Recognize that habit plays a part in your spirit of commitment. If you habitually fail to commit, fail to stick with it, fail to deliver, then you have developed a bad habit of not committing. If you habitually find yourself making excuses for not delivering, you will become very skillful at preparing excellent excuses. But is that the skill you want to become known for?

In order to be trusted in big things, you must first demonstrate that you can be trusted in small things. There is no obligation too small that it isn't important whether it gets done or not.

Commitment is not the same thing as being strong-willed, although it has something in common with it. Being strong-willed describes someone who habitually imposes their will onto others. Commitment is about being strong-willed with *yourself.* It's about imposing your will on *your* weaknesses and your tendency to slough off, be lazy, or be self-centered. Commitment could better be described as determination, resolve, or perseverance.

You may ask what trust, and the commitment aspect of trust, have to do with achieving financial success. There are, first of all, the opportunities that will come your way because you have built a reputation of being trustworthy—you do what you say you will do. This could include job promotions, contracts, even the growth of your network of friendships.

Secondly, and perhaps more important, is the strength of character you will be building when you strive to do what you say you will do—when you keep your promises. This will even benefit you in the commitments you make to yourself. When you plan to do something, set a goal, and establish a personal deadline, you have just made a commitment to yourself. If you follow through in spite of challenges and get it done, you have just strengthened your commitment "muscles." Each time you follow through, for yourself or others, you are reinforcing a good and positive habit.

On the other hand, if you only pursue your personal goals half-heartedly, without a sense of commitment, you're reinforcing a bad habit of not committing. You're building and reinforcing your own expectations of yourself. Thus, you have the power to either grow or to weaken your sense of commitment with each promise kept or broken.

Your sense of commitment is perhaps the most important aspect of trust. Don't take it lightly. If you don't think you can follow through on something, don't commit to it. By committing to small things and then following through and getting them done, you will be strengthening and growing your personal capacity for commitment. You become what you habitually do. Remember, this applies to the commitments you make to yourself as well as to others.

In addition to being honest and competent, earning trust requires that you be committed. Your sense of commitment demonstrates not only what you *can* do, but what you *will* do. This is perhaps the most important facet of trust. You look for it in others. They look for it in you. Don't disappoint them.

Chapter 22

Principle of Being Trustworthy

"It is easier to do a job right
than to explain why you didn't."

—Martin Van Buren

PRINCIPLE 18:
If You Are Not Trustworthy,
You Won't Be Trusted.

Okay, this is where we get personal. We have discussed that there are *dishonest* people in the world and that you need to acknowledge this fact and keep your guard up. We reviewed the importance of trusting that at least some people in the world are honest and, therefore, people of *character*. We noted that if you don't trust anyone, you will probably not be successful or happy. We saw that trust has an important component of *competence*. You must believe that someone is capable of doing what they say they will do. Finally, we looked at the third component of trust—*commitment*, or a determination to get done what you said you would.

The final principle to discuss now regarding trust requires you to look inward. As discussed earlier, to be successful you must accurately evaluate character, competence, and commitment in others. But just as important, you must look inward and assess how trustworthy *you* are.

Are you honest? Do you ever try to lie or color a statement so it sounds true, but it really isn't? Do you find yourself often making excuses for why something didn't get done? Do you seem to come up with really good excuses (you call them "reasons") for why you weren't able to do what you said you would do? That is not a good sign. Other people don't want to hear "good" excuses.

They want results.

There are many nice, thoughtful, loving people who are as honest as the day is long. But if they don't deliver, if they don't get done what they say they will do, what will happen? People will gradually stop trusting them, not because they are dishonest, but because they are not reliable. You can't count on them to get things done. Slowly but inevitably, people will shift their expectations and begin asking them to do less and less for them. They will turn to others whom they feel they can trust.

True competence with commitment means you don't have to be reminded by someone else to do what you said you would do. You take care of adding it to your calendar, in whatever form you do that, so that you *will* remember. It means you consider it important if you tell someone you will do something. You have just given them "your word." You have made a promise that it will happen. If you don't get it done, for whatever reason, you have failed to deliver on your promise and your commitment.

If you demonstrate time after time that you are trustworthy—honest, competent, and committed—by actually getting done what you said you would do, you will build a deep reservoir of trust on the part of others who work with you. As mentioned earlier, that will result in them honoring you with more opportunities to do things with them, whether that means giving you bigger assignments, greater responsibility, or faster promotions.

As a side note, being trustworthy will also extend into, and enhance, your personal life. Others will generally feel they can trust you. They will be more willing to share—to *entrust*—you with personal information, believing that you will not break their trust by sharing it with others.

Note the interesting phenomenon of "honor among thieves." Even criminals recognize that in order to form a successful enterprise, they must gather people around them whom they can trust. That may seem to be an oxymoron—trustworthy thieves—but it makes sense. If each person in a gang is always trying to cheat and discredit the others, how successful do you think they will be? Not very. The goals they are all trying to achieve may be very dishonorable, but in order to work together successfully in planning and carrying out a criminal endeavor, they have to trust one another to get their part of the plan done.

What happens if you do something *dishonest*? The trust others have in you will be fractured. Let's view your trustworthiness as though it were a vase sitting on a stand. As long as you continue to be trustworthy—doing what you say you will do—the vase remains beautiful and firmly placed. When you do something that damages that trust, it is as though the vase has tipped over, fallen to the floor, and shattered into pieces. When you begin working to rebuild that trust, it's like picking up all of those pieces and trying to carefully cement them back together. It takes time and perseverance, but it can possibly be done. However, the cracks will still remain. Their level of trust in you won't quite be the same.

Why is that? Because when you were dishonest, you caused them to become skeptical and uneasy about your true intentions. They now must deal with the niggling doubt that, no matter what you say or do, you may be feeling something completely different inside. You may be hiding something about your true nature. That doubt can be *very* difficult to overcome. You *may* get back to a point of being completely trusted by them again, but it can take a long time—years, perhaps.

Be sure you are not dishonest in your dealings with others! "What goes around, comes around." Dishonesty is *highly* risky. You risk losing the *trust* of those you respect, admire, and love.

In order to be financially successful, people have to feel that they can trust you. That means they believe you will be honest with them, that you are capable of doing what you say you're going to do, and that you will do whatever it takes to get it done. You will make it happen. You will fulfill your responsibilities. You will be trustworthy—and trusted.

Principles
About Vision

I n order to create something, you must have a picture in your mind of what you're aiming for—the end product. This is true in almost every creative endeavor. Building a house, cooking a special dish, accomplishing a fundraising project, and any creative hobby—knitting, crocheting, woodworking, painting—all require having a clear idea of the end product before the creative process begins.

These examples of creative pursuits illustrate the importance of having an idea, a vision, of the desired goal. This is equally important in accomplishing your financial goals. That would include not only your vision of what you hope to achieve financially in the next year, but also longer-term goals, even as long as your lifetime.

The next chapter will discuss the importance of having a vision for your life, including your finances. That's followed by a chapter addressing the importance of developing your *own* personal vision and not simply accepting someone else's.

Chapter 23

Principle of the Power of Vision

"If you don't know where you are going,
any road will get you there."

—Lewis Carroll

PRINCIPLE 19:
A Strongly Held Vision Is a Powerful
Beacon to Attract Success.

Much of the time you know where you're going without thinking about it and without needing a map. If you're going to Walmart to buy milk and bread, you know where Walmart is in your neighborhood, so you can immediately go there. That's like all of the places you go to every day, automatically, without thinking. You already know where your house is, where you work, your favorite place to buy a hamburger, and the box where you keep the ink pens at home. You can find all of the routine places or destinations that make up your life because you have been to them many, many times previously. You know where to go.

But if you want to go someplace new, say, on a vacation, then you first must decide *where* you want to go. Your destination may be a stream in which to fish, a mountain to climb, a specialty antique store, or the Metropolitan Museum of Art. It could be anyplace, anywhere. I think it's fair to say that setting your lifetime goals for your career and your finances would also be someplace new for you. You haven't yet lived your life. You don't know for certain what life will be like for you in five years, ten years, or more. It is someplace new. It will therefore require you to think about and decide where you want to be in the future regarding your life and your finances. How to do that? Let's look at how you might decide on a new vacation destination and see if there are any parallels you can apply to setting financial goals.

A VACATION VISION

Let's say you decide you would like to go to the beach, but you don't clarify that goal any further. Then, strictly speaking, any beach, anywhere in the world would fit your criteria. It could be a beach in any country, perhaps even in a frigid region, or a more hot, equatorial country. Yet if this were pointed out to you, you might reply, "Well, I meant somewhere on the coast of the US." But that still leaves it pretty wide open. Then what do you do next?

You begin to research, in broad terms, the beaches of both coasts of the US. You start considering other factors, like how far it is from your home and how long it would take to get there. You assess what the weather is like up and down both coasts and decide to narrow it down to Southern California or Florida. Good. Now you weigh other factors, like that one of your cousins lives in Georgia, so you could see them on the way to Florida. You note that the traffic in Southern California is unappealing to you, so you decide Florida it is. Now, you're going to Florida. Where in Florida? What are you going to do? How long will you stay there? How much will it cost? And so on . . .

Eventually, you decide on exactly where you want to go, which may include several cities and tourist stops. You have now developed your *vision* of your vacation destination.

In this same way you must assess, step by step, what you want out of life—what you expect to achieve and how, which would include your goals regarding finances. You start from a broad, open look at all of the options, then gradually narrow them down until you have distilled out your own personal, long-term goals for your life.

Goal-setting like this may seem daunting and perhaps unnecessary. But if you put so much thought and planning into defining your destination for a simple vacation, wouldn't it be advisable to put at least as much effort into deciding your desired destination for your career or your finances? Remember, if you don't know where you are going, then you won't know how to get there.

In our lives, we often have someplace we want to go, or think we want to go. It may be a relationship we want to grow into a marriage. It may be a long-term goal of working in a specific career. It may be an academic goal of getting a particular degree. It could include living in a certain city or in a certain type of house. In all of these instances, we have to first decide what it is we want. If we know we want to go on a vacation but we don't know where, there isn't a map in the world that can show us the way. But that's sometimes exactly what we do in our personal lives. We know we want our life to be better, but we don't think seriously about exactly *what* we would like to be better or different.

On the other hand, if we force ourselves to sit down, get quiet, and carefully reflect on what we want in a specific aspect of our lives, then, as that becomes clear to us, we can begin to seek or develop a map to show us how to get there. But only then is it useful and practical to start looking through the "box of maps" for one that will show us the way. We have to first decide our goal, our destination, before trying to assess the best way to get there.

Just as in choosing where to take a vacation, there are many different destinations that can all be called financial success. Only you can define exactly what your destination looks like. This book, and many other publications like it, can show you a lot of different financial success destinations, but you have to pick out the one, or the few, that are a unique fit for you.

It's easy to get caught up in the details of daily living and lose sight of the bigger picture. Then, when life gets especially busy, you can feel like you're floundering. If you have a clear vision of where you're heading and regularly remind yourself of that and refresh it in your mind, it will both help you to stay on track, headed toward your goal, and also decrease your stress level, because it might temporarily look like you aren't going anywhere, but you know you have a bigger picture in mind.

Sometimes a sailboat has to tack back and forth in order to make headway against the wind. If you look at the boat's position and direction at any one moment in time, it might seem like it's not heading toward the destination at all. But the master sailor, who is piloting the craft, knows what he's doing, so he both checks and manages the ongoing details of setting the sails, watching his heading, and avoiding any obstacles or hazards in the water. But he also regularly looks out into the distance at his target—

his destination—so that he keeps both the minute-by-minute corrections and the ultimate goal in mind.

It's not impossible, but it's very hard to achieve something without first being able to visualize it. If you don't know where you want to end up, whether in a relationship, a job, or your retirement financial status, how can you develop a map to show you the way to get there? Without a target destination, how will you decide even what direction to go, much less how far? You will wander aimlessly. You will find many things and places as you go through life, and some of them may actually be interesting, good, and helpful. But you will not get to a place where you are happy unless it's through blind, random luck. Don't leave out this important step of *clarifying a vision* of your financial success. It can be a great help to you as you navigate the sometimes choppy waters of life.

Chapter 24

Principle of Owning a Positive Personal Vision

"Don't set your goals by what other people deem important."

—Jaachynma N. E. Agu

PRINCIPLE 20:
Have Your Own Positive Personal Vision, Not Someone Else's.

W e form our initial vision of life based upon the visions of those who raised us. As a child, we are told what acceptable behavior is—a vision of what we should aspire to attain or become. As a teenager, we tend to want to throw out the visions that have been given to us up to that point, not realizing we have simply traded them for the collective visions of our peer group.

Our first real stab at developing our own vision may be when we are within a year or two of high school graduation. For the first time, we are asked to develop our own vision in a major way. What career do we want to pursue, and what do we need to do in order to prepare for that career? Do we go on to college, and, if so, what do we major in? Do we want to move to another area of the country for work or stay in our hometown? Lots of things to decide.

Some students seem to be filled with a vision of their desired career from a young age. That usually means they have been exposed to someone who works in that field, so they have an idea what that occupation includes. It's also possible that it's simply due to all the information they have taken in thus far in their lives, which has been enough for them to decide their career objective.

Others, even after they graduate from high school, still struggle to know what to do next. Sometimes they begin working somewhere at whatever job they can find in their local area. Occasionally, they may find they enjoy the work and the company and stay with them until they retire.

Although it may be difficult and challenging, I encourage you to seek to develop your own vision for your life. That would include your desired career, relationships, finances, and all of the other important aspects of life. You need to weigh and reflect upon the visions you have been given since your youth, then take the step of deciding your own *personal* vision.

As discussed in the previous chapter, this will enable you to rise above the daily noise of life and keep your eye on the ultimate goal: your vision for your life. It will also enlist your subconscious in helping you accomplish that. Let's elaborate on that a bit. The subconscious can be a powerful influence in achieving your vision, but it can also work against you if you aren't careful.

There is a group of success thinkers and writers who consider the subconscious to be very important. They ascribe to the theory that when your conscious mind clearly envisions a desired goal, your subconscious begins to work to bring it about. The theory is that your subconscious does not use any judgment. If you consciously envision something as though it has already happened, then your subconscious assumes it must be true and therefore begins to work to change your current situation to help bring it about—to make your vision and your current reality match up completely.

Sometimes, though, we can unwittingly plant a harmful vision into our subconscious. Let me explain. If you find yourself thinking negative thoughts about yourself, such as, *What an idiot I am. I should have known better than to have done that*, then you've just told your subconscious that you're an idiot. Remember, the theory states that your subconscious does not use any judgment. If your conscious mind says you're an idiot, your subconscious assumes that must be true. So it begins to nudge you to do things that an idiot would do! That powerful reinforcement can apply to any of the many negative things we can tell ourselves. This is sometimes called "negative self-talk," and as we all know, we can each be our own harshest critic.

This means that you must remain extremely conscious of the power of vision, both for good and for harm. Be especially vigilant to monitor and watch out for negative self-talk, because that's expressing a *vision* of yourself. If you want to be an idiot, then let yourself declare that in your mind, and you will unleash your subconscious to begin dutifully working to bring it about. But none of us *wants* to be an idiot, so you have to watch for any self-talk that expresses a vision you do *not* want for yourself. You must reject it. So when negative self-talk pops up, as it will persistently try to do, you must just as persistently shut it down and tell yourself, "No, I am not an idiot. I am smart, capable, and have a good plan that I am working toward—my vision—that does not include me being an idiot."

In summary, you must develop *your own* positive vision of where you want to go in your career, your relationships, your home life, and in your finances. This vision should be uniquely yours and should help you grow into your best self. I encourage you to develop a vision that is ambitious. Aim high. Strive to be the best you can be.

Section Seven

Principles About Obstacles

T his book would not be complete without looking at principles related to falling short, to missing the mark. These principles can help you both understand and overcome the challenges in life that work against you in your quest for success. Sometimes, in spite of our best efforts, it can seem like we are working against ourselves. Let's explore three ways we might do that and try to shed some light on how to successfully deal with them.

(Please refer to Appendix 2 for a list of common hurdles to accomplishing financial success.)

Chapter 25

Principle of Failure

*"A friend of mine says he grins every time he fails at
something. To him, failing is discovering a method that
won't work, and it brings you one step closer to succeeding.
Find many methods that don't work and one day, you'll find
a method that does. Seen this way, failure is almost the
same as success."*

—Fumio Sasaki

PRINCIPLE 21:
Setbacks and Failures Are Inevitable, Useful, and Important.

I f you've never failed, despite doing all you could to get it right, you may wish to skip this chapter, for you have been fortunate among humankind if that's the case. But if you have indeed known the discouragement and despair that comes with failing, then perhaps I can offer some encouragement. Please read on.

As with all of life, when you do something enough times, eventually you'll have a setback—you will fail at what you attempted. That's a natural part of learning and growth. In fact, that's exactly how we learn—we observe what doesn't work and what does. That's as true of the baby learning to walk as it is for the young apprentice developing the skill to build a house. The only way to never fail is to never attempt anything, and that would be a form of failure, too, wouldn't it?

No one likes the idea of failing. We all want to succeed at whatever we attempt, including how we manage our finances. But perhaps we can come to see failure as a good teacher for us.

Failure can be broadly defined as not hitting what you were aiming at—having a goal and not achieving it. Note that this could be about anything, but certainly it can include the financial aspects of your life. The key is responding to that "failure experience" so that it benefits you rather than harms you.

It has often been said that only 10 percent of success is determined by what happens to you, while 90 percent of success is determined by how you *respond* to what happens to you. I would suggest that your response to failure largely depends upon your mindset—the way you perceive, absorb, and ultimately apply the experiences of life. You could think of your mindset as how you look at the world and what you expect from it. This is the "lens" through which you view everything that happens to you, financially related or not. Another term used to describe this would be your "paradigm," a fifty-cent word that defines it even more exactly. Although there are as many different paradigms as there are individuals, I believe they broadly fall into one of two categories—a "failure" mindset or a "success" mindset. Let's take a look first at the failure mindset.

Failure Mindset

This could generally be described as having a pessimistic outlook. This is characterized by you expecting that things will *not* work out well—that you will fail. Then, when failure does happen, as it inevitably will occasionally, you believe that your feelings and expectations were vindicated. "See," you say to yourself, "I knew it wasn't going to work. I don't have . . ." or "I don't know . . ." or "I didn't think about . . ." You can fill in the blanks. The key here is that you *expected* to fail, and you let the experience of failure reinforce those expectations so that they will be even stronger the next time you attempt something.

What's the result of having a failure mindset? Typically, you will experience some, or all, of the following feelings at some point in your life:

- Negativity
- Hopelessness
- Self-pity
- Apprehension
- Loss of self-confidence
- Focusing on the past
- Self-recrimination
- Fear
- Feeling not that your *task* failed, but that *you* are a failure

None of these are helpful to you, other than perhaps motivating you to want to change. They certainly don't bring to mind thoughts of success. Rather, they bear down on the feelings associated with failure, with falling short. They make your next effort *less* likely to succeed rather than more likely to be successful.

Success Mindset

Now let's examine a success mindset and see how it differs from the failure mindset. First of all, this could broadly be described as optimism, which is pretty much the polar opposite of pessimism. When you have this mindset, you expect things to work out well. You expect to succeed. When you fail, you see it as an opportunity to learn something that doesn't work; therefore you mentally adjust and try a different approach. Perhaps most important of all, you view your successes or failures as *activities that you undertake, not as a statement of who you are*. You accept the fact that setbacks will happen, but you don't let them define you. You see them simply as obstacles to be overcome.

What's the result of having a success mindset? In contrast to the failure mindset, you will be more likely to experience the following feelings as you go through life:

- Positivity
- Excitement
- Optimism
- Hope
- Self-confidence
- Belief in yourself
- Peace
- Focus on the future

These feelings well *help* you in your quest for success. They fill you with encouragement and confidence. They empower you to persevere because you know that success will come if you keep trying different things, learning from each attempt that doesn't work out well. They will result in your small successes building on one another to create an overall feeling of being successful. This will definitely help you to be more likely to succeed on the next thing you attempt.

Perhaps the most famous example of persistence in the face of failure is Thomas Edison and his efforts to create the first incandescent light bulb. He reportedly failed over 10,000 times before he finally found the right combination of factors to create a light bulb that would successfully burn brightly for hours. As he was going through the process, you could say that he was failing, or even that *he* was a failure. What if he had quit after

9,000 attempts and given up? Then we would say that he did indeed fail, and we would never have learned about Thomas Edison. He would have simply added his name to the list of others who had attempted to create a light bulb and failed. Who knows how many others attempted to create a workable light bulb and gave up after 100, 1000, or 5000 attempts? But Edison persevered in the face of extremely daunting circumstances until he finally succeeded.

Build a Success Mindset

So how do you cultivate a success mindset rather than a failure mindset? First, you must be open to the concept that you can *choose* how you respond to what happens to you. You do not have to be subject to the whims of your feelings. When something happens to you, big or small, you have a space of time between when the event occurs and when your response happens. In that small interval of time, you can let your *mind* determine how you respond, not your feelings. This may seem impossible at first, but with practice, you can make progress at it. Decide ahead of time how you'll respond when things don't work out like you hoped. You thereby prep yourself to have the right mindset—deliberately determining, and even rehearsing, how you will respond when you fail. You mentally practice responding in a positive way.

Second, surround yourself with a supportive group of friends and family who will encourage you in your efforts to be successful. Assess who you currently have as your inner circle of friends.

Think for a minute about how they respond to life. You probably have friends who have a failure mindset and others who have a success mindset. Who do you admire the most? Who do you most enjoy being with? Who has attained the most success in life? It's important to reflect on the mindset of your friends because it's a widely held notion that you tend to become like those with whom you associate. My encouragement would be for you to think about your circle of friends and weigh whether they help you feel more optimistic and successful, or more pessimistic and unsuccessful. I propose to you that it will make a difference if you can gradually change your friends to be those who exemplify a success mindset. Those friends will also appreciate and value your success mindset because you will also be a benefit and encouragement to them!

Set Wise Goals

You can also foster a success mindset by consciously and deliberately managing the tasks, projects, or goals you set for yourself. Have you ever heard the expression that someone was "setting themselves up for failure?" There is truth in that. If you attempt to accomplish something so big, so difficult, and so challenging that it will be almost impossible to achieve, you are, in fact, setting yourself up for failure. You must use wisdom in deciding what to attempt. Setting aside some savings each month is a worthy goal, for example, but if you haven't been saving *anything* up until now, and you attempt to suddenly begin saving 25 percent of your take-home pay, you're setting yourself up for failure. What you must do is be wise and prudent about the goals you set. Make them smaller, something you can actually accomplish. Then, when you *do* succeed, that little success is an encouragement to you, rather than the discouragement that comes with failing.

As another example, if you make your to-do list for each day too long, you virtually guarantee you won't get everything on the list done. Then, at the end of the day, from one perspective you could say that you failed because you didn't succeed in getting everything on your list done. But from another perspective, look at how much you *did* get done! Thus, even something as simple as your daily to-do list can encourage or discourage you, depending on what you include in that list.

As part of setting any goals, also keep in mind the amount of risk involved. The greater the risk that you won't attain your goal, the greater the likelihood of failure. I'm not saying you should never take any risks, but do so carefully and with forethought. If you have a high-risk task you want to get done, break it down into smaller subtasks until you can easily visualize how to accomplish each of them. This lowers the risk that you won't get them finished. You want to increase the chance of having many small successes, rather than many failures. If you're unsure of how to deal with risk, take another look at chapter 7, which discusses risk in more detail.

As one more thought on goal-setting, let me share a well-known guideline from the business world: create goals that are smart. It may seem obvious that we would want to create smart goals, but do we always do that? Unfortunately, we often sabotage ourselves by creating weak or vague goals. For example, we may set a goal to "be better" at how we respond to something or to "do better" or "do more" regarding a particular task. The problem with this approach is knowing when you have accomplished it. When are you "better" enough to call it success?

A more effective approach is to set goals where it will be crystal clear whether you have succeeded or not. A vague goal would be to decide to "invest more" in this next year. A more specific goal would be to "research your options and invest $100 each month in your IRA account with TD Ameritrade over the next twelve months."

SMART is actually an acronym that can help you remember the characteristics of a "smart goal." In this common business acronym, SMART stands for:

- Specific
- Measurable
- Achievable
- Realistic
- Timely

If your goal fails to meet any of these criteria, it will be more difficult to achieve, and it will be harder to know when you have achieved it.

Perfectionism

A comment about perfectionism is needed here. If you are one who realizes you tend to be a perfectionist, then this is for you. If you assume a perfectionist outlook, what happens when you attempt something, and the results are good but not "perfect?" You minimize, or even outright ignore, the good results that occur. Instead, you find yourself obsessing over any small aspects of the results that were not perfect. You *force* yourself to conclude that you failed. What a harsh taskmaster is this perfectionist streak! Of course, the definition of perfection can also be modified at any time to ensure that it is so exact, so complete, that it can never be attained!

So, what to do?

I would suggest that at some point in your past, you were subjected to unrealistic expectations. To someone important in your life, no matter how hard you tried or how well you did, it was never good enough. If you made straight As on your report card except for one B, for example, then the focus and emphasis was on that solitary B rather than the overall exemplary report card. As a result, you may have absorbed the feeling that you don't deserve to succeed—you deserve to fail. So with dogged perfectionism, you make sure that your work can't be considered a success.

If you can come to see how that might be the case for you, then half the battle to overcome perfectionism is won. Otherwise, you don't even realize there is a battle to be fought! Having high standards is commendable. Having unrealistically high, perfectionistic standards is a guaranteed recipe for a feeling of failure. I encourage you to let yourself succeed. You are a worthwhile human being who deserves to enjoy success as much as anyone else.

Keeping a Success Mindset

To wrap up this chapter, I would like to share a story with you. This is one that can be applied to all of us, to one degree or another. It deals with the ever-present trap of slipping back into a failure mindset. You may find the story humorous, but the warning is serious and can hopefully help you guard against any attack on your success mindset.

THE FAILURE MERCHANT

We each have a "Failure Merchant" inside our mind who tries to ride around with us all day, every day, wherever we go. He appears to be an intelligent fellow and someone to be trusted. He is dressed in a nice business suit and looks very professional. When we examine him more closely, though, we can see his true colors. His hair is oily and slicked down, smooth and black. When he smiles, there is a gold tooth visible, evidence of a crude repair from a past battle he lost. Perhaps the most telling feature is his eyes. They appear soft and blue at first, but when we hold his gaze, we realize they glitter with a startling hardness and ruthlessness. There is no compassion in those eyes.

He is continually trying to sell you his message, his lie—that you are a failure. He has nothing else to do except jump up and begin yammering at you anytime you look in his direction. He takes on many forms and approaches—whatever might work at the time. He can be smooth and soothing, or raw, blunt, and vicious. He is an expert at weaseling himself into your thoughts, always looking for any small little slipup on which to pounce. He will gleefully point it out to you as evidence that you are indeed a failure. "You might as well give up!" he demands.

But he also realizes that you can *choose* whether you buy his bill of goods or not. His underlying strategy is to keep you from recognizing that. If *you* don't realize you can choose whether to accept what he says or not, you submissively absorb whatever lie he's trying to sell you as though you have no alternative but to do so. That's what he's counting on. Once you're aware that you can resist him, then his power is dramatically diminished. You have set him back on his heels, and he'll be scrambling to try and poke holes in the notion that you don't have to listen to him. He may even be forced to retreat altogether, waiting for another opportune time to jump back into your conscious mind.

It's important to recognize that it's easy to slip back into a failure mindset when you experience a setback. You naturally feel disappointment at your lack of success, and that can work against you if you let it. If you can keep this Failure Merchant analogy in mind, though, then you'll see him as someone to be consciously opposed. You can then more easily keep that feeling of being a failure at bay. That can inspire you to resist him. Don't listen to him. You are a success!

Setbacks are inevitable. Expect them. Embrace them. View them not as failure but as learning and growth opportunities and as a critical part of the learning process. Stay engaged in life. Keep trying. You were built and engineered for success. Let it happen.

Chapter 26

Principle of Regret

"I think it's never too late to start anything,
except maybe being a ballerina."

—Wendy Liebman

PRINCIPLE 22:
Regret Must Be Tamed, Lest It Eat Alive All Chances for Success.

I f you order a cheeseburger when out to lunch with a friend, then you see how delicious the pulled pork looks on your friend's plate, you may *regret* not ordering the pulled pork. But how long will you experience that feeling of regret? A few minutes at most, and then the conversation moves on and you promptly forget about it. (If you continue to regret getting the cheeseburger, though, I do understand. I love pulled pork!)

The kind of regret I am talking about concerns bigger issues in life.

The previous chapter talked about failure. The idea put forth was that everyone fails from time to time. In response, you should assess what went wrong, decide to make a change in your behavior, correct anything damaged, and then move on. But sometimes the failure can be so big, and the pain so cutting, that the failure continues to replay itself over and over in your mind. That's a key characteristic of regret. It happened in the past, but you keep pulling it back into the present, bringing with it all of the feelings that were associated with that failure. You're keeping the failure fresh and alive in your mind. Your brain or your heart just can't seem to let go of it.

You may have attempted to correct any harm you caused. You worked to make amends if your failure caused pain, loss, or hurt to others. You apologized if needed. You restored anything that you may have damaged or taken. You have already done all of those things, and have corrected the situation to the best of your ability. Yet you still feel the fresh pain of what happened, and of what you lost.

With regret, we experience a sense of loss because of what we said or did. This could be the loss of respect from someone we admire, a financial loss, an opportunity lost, the loss of a friendship, or other losses. Basically, though, we are acutely aware that we have *lost* something, and we assume we can never get it back. Closing the barn door now won't help. The horses are already out.

What are some situations that can prompt feelings of regret? There can be many, but here are just a few:

- The person deeply in debt
- The person who has squandered opportunities
- The person who rejected others who were trying to help him or her
- The person who has spent far too much on a major purchase

Let me offer a more detailed example. Perhaps you always wanted to be a teacher when you were young. Your family didn't have enough funds to send you to college, so you became a landscaper. You have now been doing landscaping for twenty years and have established a good career. But you still regret not trying harder to find some way to get your degree and become a teacher, your real career ambition.

Perhaps you have failed to save regularly and are now at retirement age and have very little set aside for retirement. You regret that you didn't get serious about saving earlier in life, but it seems that it's too late to do anything about it now.

There can be many, many things in your past that can live on as regret. Each of us can have our own unique set of past circumstances and actions that result in us feeling that way. But whatever the cause, the result is that regret brings with it a sense of hopelessness. "Why try? It's no use. I'm just a failure, and there's nothing I can do about it now. That was such a big mistake that I can never overcome it. I totally blew it. I am toast."

If you want to get rid of your feelings of regret, what can you do?

First of all, you must come to recognize that your regret is not serving a good purpose. Does it help your state of mind to wallow in regret? Does it change your situation? No, it only serves to make you miserable. It takes away your motivation and your confidence to try again. It steals your joy. Your regret is not helping you; instead, it's hurting you.

I suggest that you actually view regret as an enemy. Remember the Failure Merchant from the previous chapter? He uses regret as one of his favorite weapons. It is well-worn and shiny from use. It's as though he is sneering and saying, "Well, you thought you could achieve this grand vision of yours, but let me show you what happened when you tried to do that. You failed! So you just might as well give up! You will never succeed in accomplishing that vision!" He (regret) is your enemy. Oppose him!

You must also recognize that you have to change your behavior. If you're still continuing the actions that prompted you to get into your current situation, then your situation is not going to change until you change. If you regret having $8,000 of credit card debt, you must change the way you spend your money. If you don't, then you will continue to have a high credit card balance. It's also important to realize that *you* control whether you change your attitude, your habits, and your practices of saving and spending.

Since regret is an emotion, you must consciously replace it with a stronger, overriding, positive emotion. In order to push down one feeling, you must have another ready to replace it. If you don't, then when you remove the regret from your life, it leaves a hole. If you don't have something to put back into that hole, it will act like a vacuum and pull regret right back into your consciousness.

Gratitude may be the best candidate for filling that hole. Let's consider it.

Step back and reflect on your life, trying to look for the positive. In spite of challenges, we all have some good in our lives. When living in a modern, developed country, we forget the many basic amenities we enjoy—running water, electricity, the Internet, air-conditioning, the automobile, and so on. If you can remind yourself of the blessings, however small, that you have experienced in your life, then your regret can gradually be replaced by gratitude. Remember, though, it's up to you to decide what you focus on. The glass can be half full or half empty, but it's still the same glass. A situation doesn't change; only the way you view it changes.

You also have to forgive yourself.

We usually think of forgiveness as something we do in response to what someone else did to us. But it can also be us forgiving ourselves for something we did in our past. It may have been something stupid, thoughtless, selfish, hurtful, or arrogant. Whatever it was, if we're sorry about it and *regret* that we did it, that shows contrition. In effect, we need to "ask" ourselves for forgiveness. We may find that hard or awkward to do, but it is necessary. We need to be kind to our past self. We were doing the best that we could at that point in our life with who we were and what we knew about the situation. That's not only the way we need to view the failings of others, but also our own failings.

Basically, we need to let the cycle be completed. Allow me to explain.

When we feel regret, we are sorrowful about something we did. We, in effect, are repentant. We remind ourselves that our first step was to fix or repair the damage that resulted from our failure. Now it's time for us to forgive ourselves. Otherwise, we remain stuck in the repentant stage, repeatedly saying, "I am sorry! I am sorry! I am sorry!" We are like an old LP record player, stuck in a damaged groove in the record, repeating the same phrase over and over. When you forgive yourself, it's like nudging the arm of the record player ever so gently, which bumps the arm out of the groove, allowing the rest of the record to continue to play the beautiful music stored on it. That is like letting yourself move on with your life and resuming the music of your life story. It doesn't change the fact that the scratched groove still remains on the record. That failure is still in your past. But the difference is that you're no longer stuck in it. You resume playing your life song.

You also have to be careful and vigilant for the first few weeks after you forgive yourself. If you aren't careful, you will find you have picked the record player arm up and moved it back to that damaged groove. You're stuck once again! To get out, you may need to forgive yourself—again.

Maybe you feel you don't deserve to be forgiven. For a different perspective on that, let's look at a situation involving you forgiving someone else. If your child or a close friend does something hurtful, but then is sorry afterward, do they always *deserve* for you to forgive them? Maybe or maybe not, but if you love them, you do it. Forgiveness, in that case, is your way of saying that what was done damaged your relationship, but you value both them and the relationship. You want to restore that relationship, so you forgive them. That is exactly what we must do with ourselves.

We must also be firm with the Failure Merchant, or he will keep selling us his lies, getting us to believe they are something that can never change. Remember that his goal is to make you as miserable and ineffective as possible. But he needs your permission to do so! You can refute what he says and, in effect, close the door in his face, removing him and his influence over your daily life. But you must *consciously and deliberately* choose to do that. He loves to sneak up and whisper into your subconscious until you naively take up the same chant that he is spewing—that you are a failure, that you can't recover from what you did, that you might as well give up.

Eleanor Roosevelt stated, "No one can make you feel inferior without your permission."[19] The same is true with regret. Regret is something that is all yours. It is internal. No one else can make you feel regret. Only you can. In the same way, no one else can take away your feeling of regret either. Again, only you can.

As we go through life, we all make mistakes. We are human. To live a successful life, financially and in every other way, requires that we view those mistakes properly. If we continue to relive them, keeping ourselves soaked with regret, we hinder our ability to move on with our life. We must consciously reject the accusations of the

Failure Merchant, take any restorative actions that are needed, forgive ourselves, and focus on the good in our life. It's never too late to start living by the principles of financial success. Today is the first day of the rest of your life.

Chapter 27

Principle of Comfort Zone

"Life always begins with one step outside of your comfort zone."

—Shannon L. Alder

PRINCIPLE 23:
Our Psyche Is Loath to Move out of Our Comfort Zone.

O nce you have decided to make a change, or changes, in how you manage your personal finances, you may discover that it will require you to move outside of your comfort zone. That factor can be a subtle but very strong influence that will resist the change you're attempting. We must learn how to deal with our comfort zone and its effect on us, or it can undo all of our good intentions and efforts. Let's look at the concept of our comfort zone, what it is, and how we might productively deal with it.

We all begin life with the smallest of comfort zones: the womb of our mother. Sheltered there in her warmth, we are completely content. Then comes that traumatic day of birth, and the cozy, dark womb is behind us. We are faced with lights, noises, cool air, voices, and movement all around us. We are terrified! Our comfort zone has been suddenly and dramatically expanded, whether we were ready for it or not. Fortunately, we soon sense the warm body and soothing words of our mother, and we gradually adjust. Our comfort zone stretches outward to include these new faces, sounds, and sights. The lifelong process of expanding our comfort zone has begun.

Your comfort zone can be described as the total collection of all of your regular life habits. It is how you live your life, most of the time, most of every day. We don't think about or discuss our comfort zone much, but we definitely do feel it. We know when an activity is pushing us outside of our comfort zone, and we unconsciously resist moving there. If you haven't done a particular activity in a proposed new way, you can feel a subtle sense of risk. When you stay in your comfort zone, you tend to feel . . . well, comfortable!

How much you value and feel compelled to stay in your comfort zone is a very personal thing, unique to you.

Some people embrace the excitement of change and new adventures, thus regularly pushing the boundaries of their comfort zone. Mountain climbers, for example, are always thinking about the next peak to scale. They want to go higher, farther, and make ever more difficult climbs, always testing the limits of their ability, of their comfort zone. If you have that type of temperament, uneasiness at stretching your comfort zone may not be an issue for you at all. You may happily opt to just move on to the next chapter.

For most of us, though, our comfort zone gives us a sense of security. We like keeping our lives within it. We find moving out of our comfort zone to be at least a little unsettling, and perhaps downright unnerving. We may even see the imagined walls of our comfort zone as protecting us from what is outside. So we prize our walls and enjoy letting them get as high, hard, and thick as possible. We see them as good and comforting. Most of the time, though, in order to make a change in our life, we have to do something that may not be easy. It may not be comfortable. It may be outside of our comfort zone.

When we are a child, our comfort zone is very small. For a baby, simply being held by someone other than their mother may trigger an outcry of fear and panic. They were moved outside of their comfort zone. As children, and then young adults, we were continually encouraged by our parents and others to expand our comfort zone, to step out and try something new.

- "Walk to Daddy! C'mon, you can do it!"
- "You will do great in the first grade. You can do it!"
- "Try out for the team. You can do it!"
- "Go for that scholarship. You can do it!"

You can do it. Words of encouragement. Words of support. Words of belief. These all gave us the courage to try, to step out past the boundary of our current comfort zone. They helped us overcome our fear of whatever we were attempting that we had not attempted before. We were steadily encouraged to expand our comfort zone.

When we begin our education in the school system, we're pushed beyond our comfort zone all the time. That's part of the process of growing up. Each year of school brings new challenges. This continues even into early adulthood, where we move beyond our comfort zone to learn new skills or a new profession, move to a new city, start a new job, or start a new relationship—all of these push us outside of our comfort zone. As a young person, you typically embrace these changes. It is invigorating and a sign of your growing adulthood.

Then, as we proceed through life, we occasionally get knocked down. Something doesn't work out like we thought it would. That person we like romantically doesn't seem to care for us at all. We tried something bold at work but still didn't get that promotion. We joined a health club and have injured ourselves. These setbacks, and others like them, have the effect of beginning to harden the walls of our comfort zone. *If I venture out beyond them, I might get hurt*, we subconsciously think. *Best to stay in here where I am comfortable.*

Fear

The primary feeling associated with moving out of your comfort zone is fear. You fear that you may fail. You fear that you may look foolish or stupid. You fear that you may get laughed at. You fear that you may be ridiculed. You fear that you may lose your job. You fear that you may destroy a friendship. You fear that you may even die (as is the case with mountain climbing)!

Our fears as an adult are no different than the fear the first grader feels as she climbs up the steps on her first day of school, or the boy trying out for the traveling baseball team, or even the high school student applying for their dream college. Fear is a universal experience that we all understand.

This fear can prevent us from breaking out of our comfort zone in a good and positive way. This can be true for even small attempts at change. Say we have had a problem with spending too much at Starbucks. We have become accustomed to having our special drink on the way to work each morning. They make it exactly the way we like it, and we view it as a little indulgence that we deserve.

But let's say you have decided that it would be good for you to spend less on coffee. You're spending roughly $25 each week, or $100 every month on Starbucks coffee. You decide that you're going to change and begin using that $100 to pay down debt rather than spend it on coffee. Is that all you have to do? Simply decide to do it, and then it will happen?

For almost every one of us, that will not be an easy change to make. Why? Because it moves us outside of our comfort zone. We fear that we will not be happy with our new Starbucks-less life. We *fear* that life will not be as good. We will have lost something of precious value. This is admittedly a softer fear than the fear of falling off a mountain, but it is real nonetheless. Think of it as skepticism, doubt, or apprehension, if that seems a more fitting description to you than fear. But note that, small or not, it can still drive our behavior.

We are prone to favor staying within our comfort zone. Why is that? Because when we have previously experienced the activities that are within our comfort zone, they felt safe and predictable. We have a good idea what will happen. If we move beyond our comfort zone, we aren't sure how things will turn out. There is now a risk that it might not turn out well. But in order to grow, to learn new skills, to take on new responsibilities, we must move the walls of our comfort zone. When we do so, and they move outward, it reveals new territory that we have never traversed. It can be scary, but it's a necessary part of growth.

We should note that just because something is *outside* of our comfort zone, that doesn't mean it's a good thing for us. There are many dangerous activities that would understandably be outside most people's comfort zones. Skydiving, scuba diving, mountain climbing, and motorcycle racing are just a few activities that are probably outside of most people's comfort zones, and for good reason.

Similarly, just because something is *within* our comfort zone doesn't mean it's good for us. Unfortunately, we can establish some bad habits, things we need to work on changing. If our comfort zone includes going to the casino every night, and we hardly have enough money for the essentials of life, then that habit, which is within our comfort zone, is clearly not good for us.

Here are some suggestions for dealing with your comfort zone when you are ready to make a change:

- Think about the change you want to make, and weigh if it is healthy, positive, and beneficial to you. If it is, let that motivate you.
- Define your comfort zone boundaries related to this change. Assess if they are appropriate or if they need to be stretched outward.
- Determine and define which areas you plan to change, and *anticipate* feeling somewhat anxious when you do so.
- Remind yourself that moving out of your comfort zone is growth. Growth is good!

Success almost always requires stepping out of your comfort zone, the place where you feel confident, competent, and *comfortable*. When you do so, you grow, you stretch your capabilities and your belief in what is possible. Moving past the boundary of your comfort zone will often prompt fear—fear of failure, ridicule, embarrassment, or one of a hundred other imagined disasters. If you expect and anticipate that feeling of fear, then you can better deal with it. Remember that living your life is your own personal adventure. When you move beyond the edge of your comfort zone, you grow and feel the excitement and anticipation of change, of stretching yourself. Be bold. Don't let your comfort zone define who you are and what you can and can't do. Remember that new pathways to success lie just outside of your comfort zone. Go for it!

Principles About Extreme Trials

I wrestled with whether to include this next section in the book. My overall goal is to be an *encouragement* to you, and this section seems to focus on abject failure. Not an encouraging topic. But if you have found yourself in that spot, seemingly at the end of your rope, you might appreciate some suggestions on how to deal with your situation.

If you feel that things can't get any worse, and you're looking for help of any kind, then read on. If you have never been at that point, then count your blessings.

Chapter 28

Principle of Hitting Bottom

"When defeat comes, accept it as a signal that your plans are not sound, rebuild those plans, and set sail once more toward your coveted goal."

—Napoleon Hill

PRINCIPLE 24:
Desperate Times Demand
Desperate Measures.

T here are many ways that someone can experience extreme loss. Life brings with it the occasional deep disappointment—perhaps the revelation of a shocking deed done by a trusted friend, the betrayal by a loved one, or a major financial setback. All of these can be devastating and may take time and courage to accept and deal with. The focus of this chapter is on *major financial* loss, or being in dire straits, financially speaking.

Many things can cause a catastrophic hit to our finances. Some may be outside of our control. A sudden job loss, a debilitating injury that robs one of his ability to practice his trade, or a natural disaster of great magnitude. These and many other negative circumstances can befall any of us through no fault of our own, but the impact to our financial life is just as real nonetheless. These disappointments can feel crushing at the time, but unless bitterness sets in, they can often be overcome through perseverance and determination.

Of a completely different nature is a financial failure that was of your own doing. There are countless ways for a person to screw up their life. Some can have a very dramatic and explosive impact, both personally and financially.

- Drug addiction
- Gambling

- Infidelity
- Theft
- Anger
- And the list goes on . . .

Other financial failures have causes that are quieter and more subtle.

- Persistently spending more than you earn
- Trying to prop up a lavish, extravagant lifestyle
- Providing much more for a relative than you can afford
- Loaning substantial money to others (family or friends) that doesn't get repaid

The bottom line: whatever the cause, you are now broke. You may no longer have a source of income. Perhaps you can't pay your basic utility bills or even afford food. You cannot provide for your family. You are close to being destitute, and you are desperate.

Extreme hardship, if nothing else, is good for getting your attention! Your focus is laser sharp as everything else in your life fades in importance when compared to "getting back on your feet" financially.

So, if you find yourself in such a situation, please read on.

First of all, it's important to analyze *why* you ended up hitting rock bottom so that you don't end up back there again. If you clearly know the reasons you are here, then you must take every step necessary to address the root causes. Otherwise, any changes you make will be like taping a bandage over a festering sore. For a time, it will be out of sight, and you will be tempted to think it's cured. But unless the sore is cleaned out, cauterized, treated with healing ointment, and *then* bandaged, it will never heal.

If it isn't clear to you why you got into this situation, I encourage you to assess which of the principles outlined in this book you are failing to live in harmony with. You may want to talk to a close friend, someone who will be loving but bluntly honest with you. It may be a flaw in your thoughts or actions that you're not able to see for yourself. Seek another's insight.

Once the underlying cause has been faced—and steps taken to address it—then you can begin the walk back to financial wholeness. Below are some suggested steps to follow.

Drastically Cut Your Costs to the Bone

You may feel that you have already done this, but I encourage you to take another look at your expenses to see what else can be cut. Pretending you don't really need to do this only prolongs the pain. You must swallow your pride and try to get your life down to the absolute essentials.

- **Food**: Eat at home, not in restaurants or in fast food places. It costs *much* more to eat meals out. Save and eat leftovers. Cook healthy, using fresh vegetables. Avoid expensive packaged food.
- **Shelter**: You need only the basic services—protection from the elements, heat, electricity, running water, inside toilet, solid walls, lockable doors, and a safe neighborhood. Consider temporarily moving in with a friend or family member. Offer to help pay something for their housing expenses, if you can.
- **Rest**: You need a clean bed to sleep in and a sense of security regarding where you are getting your rest at night.

- **Cleaning**: Establish a place to clean yourself and your clothing. A simple shower stall and used washer and dryer can probably cover that.
- **Transportation**: You might need to rely on public transportation for a time. It is often cheaper than owning a vehicle, which requires gas, maintenance, and insurance.

Do Not Borrow Additional Funds

It's very likely that excessive borrowing and expensive debt is at least part of the reason you're in your current situation. You must try hard not to add any more debt. If you absolutely must borrow more, your credit rating is probably going to be poor at this point. Therefore, you may not have many sources of lending available to you. I strongly urge you to avoid predatory lenders (discussed in chapter 14). The interest rates they charge are exorbitant. Do everything in your power not to borrow from any of these sources: payday lenders, pawn shops, loan sharks, or similar lenders. Doing so will only push you deeper into debt.

Keep the attitude that you have to *work* your way out of debt, not *borrow* your way out.

Negotiate with Your Creditors

Most lenders would rather get a small, regular payment from you than nothing at all. Communicate with them. Let them know your situation. Ask if they can accept a reduced payment for a period of time. If a lender does give you a reprieve and decreases the expected monthly payment, do everything in your power to honor and make those new payments on time, every month. If you do, you will slowly begin rebuilding credibility with that lender.

You may consider a debt consolidation loan. Just be sure to read the fine print to make sure you understand the terms. You are trying to decrease your total monthly required payments, but you are also trying to decrease the monthly interest you are paying.

Utilize Any and All Available Free Services

In most communities, there are a variety of free services available to help those in severe need. Food, clothing, and even shelter can be found, at least on a temporary basis. There are agencies that can assist with developing job skills, applying for jobs, filing taxes, debt counseling, and exploring various types of welfare available.

Government offices, both national and local, can be a source of assistance. Seek them out. Present your situation and see what they can offer you. If you have worked previously, explore filing for unemployment.

Let me warn you to be sure to keep the attitude that these free services are *temporary*. It is easy to get lulled into thinking you could live off free help from now on. That's one aspect of welfare that can be detrimental to your long-term health and happiness because it leaves you dependent rather than independent. *(Please refer to Appendix 6 for an in-depth discussion about the benefits and pitfalls of welfare.)*

Find a Source of Income

The main way to improve your financial situation is by getting a job. That is what will enable you to cover your living expenses, pay down your debt, and allow you to regain independence. This is the main thing you need to focus on. As the saying goes, aim to "keep the main thing, the main thing."

There are jobs available. Get the best one you can in the short term. It may be an undesirable and even unpleasant job, but it will bring in income, and it establishes that you are willing to work. Be a good worker. Show up every day, on time, and work hard. Pay attention to what you're tasked with doing. Then, as you work at that job, continue to explore other job opportunities. Move up to a better job when you find it, but don't quit your old job until you secure a new one.

Strive to Keep a Positive Attitude

It will understandably be difficult for you to keep a positive attitude when you're struggling to climb out of a deep financial hole. It is crucial that you strive to do so though. If you can, you will not only be helping yourself but also any others affected by your struggles, such as your family. If you *act* desperate, your family will *feel* desperate. If you act confident, your family will feel confident. Remember that you *can* be healthy and happy with very little—if you choose. This attitude will enable you to hang in there and rise out of your situation, step by step. Remind yourself that food, clothing, and shelter can be *very* basic, yet be enough to live on and provide a base to build upon as your finances slowly improve.

As a Last Resort, Declare Bankruptcy

You may come to a place where there is no other alternative but to declare bankruptcy and start over. I encourage you to view that as your last resort, but it is a valid option. The next chapter will discuss that path in more detail.

For many potential reasons, you may find yourself hitting rock bottom financially. You may feel there is no way out, and you are destined to live in poverty for the rest of your life. There are always steps that can be taken, though, to begin the slow climb back to financial independence. Analyze and understand the reasons why you ended up where you are. Decide what changes you need to make, and begin implementing them. Seek out all sources of assistance. Work hard. Live on less. Try to stay positive. You can work your way out of a pretty deep hole, but you have to start, and then you have to keep at it. Others have managed to do so; with perseverance, so can you. Reading this book and noting what needs to be changed in your financial life is a beautiful testimony to your desire and willingness to do what it takes to get your finances back on track. Hang in there. You can do it.

Chapter 29

Principle of Starting Over

"Bankruptcy is a serious decision
that people have to make."

—Herb Kohl

PRINCIPLE 25:
Bankruptcy Is a Last Resort,
Not a Resort.

W hat if you are at the point where you don't see any way you can ever pay off your debts, in spite of taking every step you can think of to improve your financial situation? What if you find yourself unable to keep up with any of the bills, much less paying down a mountain of debt? There is one more option available to you—declaring bankruptcy.

Before taking this step, I must remind you again that it is crucial to research and determine *why* you ended up on the brink of declaring bankruptcy. What did you do, or fail to do, that has resulted in this situation? Unless you accurately assess what actions caused this, you will likely end up back at this point again, and sooner rather than later. Why? Because if you take the same actions you've been taking, you will get the same results. Actions have consequences, and the same action will usually produce the same consequence.

There is a tendency to feel that circumstances beyond your control were what caused this to happen. I would gently challenge you to reconsider that point of view. For example, let's say that you or a family member has a serious and expensive medical situation, one that has resulted in significant debt. This is a common contributing cause of bankruptcy. You may feel that such a situation is clearly outside of your control. Medical issues can be one of the most discouraging because they impact you physically and emotionally. You have my sympathy if you are dealing with such a health crisis in your family.

In every situation, I think it pays to ask if there was anything you could have done to lessen the impact of it, even in a situation as challenging as a medical concern. I know this may be an emotional subject for you to consider, but please pause and allow yourself to think about how you had planned to cover any medical problems. Remember also that this is just an example. Your situation may not include medical factors at all, but the same concepts apply. I am not trying to make you feel guilty, but I am trying to help you face the situation and explore ways to change it.

Let's continue with the health challenge example. What health insurance did you have, and what was the coverage, including deductibles and limits? Did you opt out of insurance altogether, preferring to take the risk that you or your family members would not get ill? What steps did you take to maintain your health and the health of your family? Think about what things you can control. Perhaps you did everything that you could see needed to be done. My encouragement is to simply consider any other steps that could be taken to improve the situation or lessen the impact.

Moving to another example, what if you were cleaned out by a criminal scammer? "How could I have prevented that?" you may ask. Let's look at how you had prepared yourself for such a situation. What steps had you taken prior to that to educate yourself on how to spot and avoid scammers and their schemes? Did you keep your software up to date to protect against malware, ransomware, and the many other forms of harmful software? Did you ask anyone else for advice when you first began to suspect something might be amiss, or were you too embarrassed to do so?

The point is not to make you feel badly because you didn't do enough to protect yourself and those you love. The point is to help you realize that there are *always* steps that can be taken to help shelter yourself from serious financial ruin. You may not be able to avoid circumstances that come your way. Your house may catch on fire, you or a family member may contract a serious illness, or you may be targeted by online criminals. There are lots of unfortunate circumstances that can happen to any of us. Our responsibility is to think about what *might* happen, and then not only attempt to prevent it from happening, but also take steps to lessen the impact if such an event occurs. If you have adequate homeowner's insurance, including full replacement value coverage, then if your house burns down, it is an *emotional* tragedy, but it won't have to be a *financial* tragedy as well. Your insurance can cover the cost of temporary housing, rebuilding your home, and replacing all of your lost personal belongings. But that will happen only if you have the correct homeowner's insurance.

Filing for bankruptcy is a legal action that requires the assistance of an attorney. They will explain to you your options, and the pros and cons of the various avenues you could pursue. Check out the credentials of any attorney you plan to hire. Ask for references from others who have used them. You want to shop for quality service from an attorney, just as you would when you shop for anything else.

You may be tempted to view bankruptcy as a convenient bailout. You had a lot of debt; suddenly, that debt is gone! Seems like a sweet deal. Realize that there will be significant restrictions placed on you, perhaps for several years. You may not be able to get a credit card for quite a long time, for example. You may have to sell some things that you never planned to sell. It is a blessing to have the opportunity to start over, but there is pain that goes along with it.

My encouragement for you if you do declare bankruptcy is that you determine you will never let yourself get to that point again. You can eventually rebuild your financial life if you're patient and consistent in your corrective actions. But you will now always have, in the back of your mind, that bankruptcy is an option if you let yourself get into trouble again. If you choose to declare bankruptcy a second, third, or more times, your credibility will go down and your opportunity to correct your life will diminish with each succeeding bankruptcy.

My advice is to view multiple bankruptcies like multiple divorces. If you find yourself declaring divorce for the second, third, or fourth time, you may be inclined to think there just aren't any good men or women in the world. But wouldn't it be reasonable to step back and question whether *you* may be the problem? Either you are impossible to live with, or you have really bad judgment in choosing a spouse. In either case, the fault partly lies with you, not solely with your ex-spouses. In the same way, if you declare bankruptcy more than once, financial institutions, credit reporting services, and employers will become increasingly skeptical about your commitment to achieving financial stability. Life will continue to get more difficult. Remember, you are working to be *successful* in your financial life, not repeatedly declaring bankruptcy.

Bankruptcy is not a step to be taken lightly. It has serious, long-term consequences for your financial status. It is, though, a legal, viable option as a way to deal with an insurmountable debt that cannot be paid. Before deciding to declare bankruptcy, I encourage you to try the suggestions offered in the previous chapter on hitting bottom. If you still cannot see a way out of debt, then bankruptcy may be the best option for you. Remember, you must still assess what circumstances led you to this point. You must determine what changes need to be made and start making them, or you will likely end up back in bankruptcy again in a few short years.

Applying the Principles

W e're now down to the last chapter, the one that really counts. Learning about all these principles is good, but *applying* what you have learned is where the real change takes place. Reading about something is not the same as doing it. It's now decision time!

Chapter 30

Making It Happen

"Carpe diem. [Seize the day.]"

—Horace

W**e have reviewed** together many different principles related to financial success. My hope is that you have found them to be informative and helpful. The real test of that comes now. What do you plan to do?

First of all, you must decide whether to accept that these principles are true or not. If you don't believe they're true, then clearly no action is required. But if you have come to believe that some or all of them *are* true, then you are agreeing that your financial life will go better if you conform your actions to be in alignment with these truths, these principles.

Now we are down to the self-discipline part. How do you succeed in marshaling the intestinal fortitude, the "guts" to make it happen, to change from an unsuccessful approach to a successful one? I propose six things for you to consider that can help in this effort.

1) First, you must make the decision that you want to change. Once you make a clear decision, then you can begin working on implementing that decision.

2) Second, you must plan what you're going to do. Refresh your vision of your desired life and your desired financial life. Develop intermediate targets. Set a timeframe.

3) Third, you must prioritize your life. You cannot accomplish anything new unless you *don't* do some other things. There are only so many hours in the day and so many ounces of energy and concentration available to each of us every day. Something has to give.

4) Fourth, you must act! Once your plan is ready and you have determined your priorities, then you must start. You must step out. Today.

5) Keep on learning. Next year, the world will be a different place. Your life will be different. You will be different. You must keep on observing, absorbing, and growing in order to adapt and change as your world changes.

6) Keep on rolling. Stay positive. Never give up. No matter what happens, you have to just keep on rolling.

I believe in you. You can do this.

The Arena

"*It is not the critic who counts; not the man who points out how the strong man stumbles, or where the doer of deeds could have done them better. The credit belongs to the man who is actually in the arena, whose face is marred by dust and sweat and blood; who strives valiantly; who errs, who comes short again and again, because there is no effort without error and shortcoming; but who does actually strive to do the deeds; who knows the great enthusiasms, the great devotions; who spends himself in a worthy cause; who at the best knows in the end the triumph of high achievement, and who at the worst, if he fails, at least fails while daring greatly, so that his place shall never be with those cold and timid souls who neither know victory nor defeat.*"

—Theodore Roosevelt

The Most Important Thing

Perhaps you feel at this point that you can only implement one thing from this book. If you want to focus on the one change in your life that will have the greatest impact, this is it:

> Live below your means. Not just within your means,
> but **below** your means.

This will provide you with the foundation to begin controlling your spending, working your way out of debt, saving for emergencies, and growing a nest egg for retirement. Living below your means, more than anything else, will give you a sense of peace from knowing that you are controlling your finances rather than your finances controlling you.

Acknowledgments

I wish to express appreciation to all those who helped make this book possible. I couldn't have accomplished this without the dedicated and thorough work of my copy editor, Shannon Cave. She opened my eyes to new possibilities in how to express myself and helped me clean up my structure. My proofreader, Jenna Love Schrader, suggested many changes that really elevated the quality of the whole book, and kept me on the straight and narrow grammatically. The easy-to-read formatting is the handiwork of my designer, Sarah Lahay, and the beautiful cover was created by Jennifer Stimson. I am also grateful for the professional coaching and assistance from Angela Hoy and the staff at my publisher, Booklocker. I also appreciate the encouragement and insights from the Miller Writers Group in Fort Smith, Arkansas. Finally, I am most grateful for the continual support and encouragement through it all of my wife, Margaret.

The Principles of Financial Success

Principles About Life

1) "Actions Have Consequences."

2) "You Are Responsible for Your Life."

3) "Rewards Come from Managing Risk, Not Fearing It."

4) "Habits Are Either Your Servant or Your Master."

Principles About the Psychology of Money

5) "Net Worth Is One Key Measure of Financial Success—Debt Matters."

6) "Money *Will* Influence You Psychologically."

7) "You Must Understand Yourself in Order to Know What You Need."

Principles About How We Use Money

8) "You Must First Earn Before You Can Save."

9) "If You Spend Wisely, You Get More for Your Money."

10) "The Borrower Is Slave to the Lender."

11) "Spend Less Than You Earn."

12) "Investing Is Making Your Money Work for You."

13) "Giving Benefits Both the Giver and the Receiver of the Gift."

Principles About Trust

14) "There Will Always Be Dishonest People After Your Money."
15) "Honesty Is the Mortar That Binds Together the Building Blocks of Success."
16) "Knowledge and Skill Determine Competence, Not Good Intentions."
17) "A Promise Without Commitment Is a Fragile Hope Coated with Good Intentions."
18) "If You Are Not Trustworthy, You Won't Be Trusted."

Principles About Vision

19) "A Strongly Held Vision Is a Powerful Beacon to Attract Success."
20) "Have Your Own Positive Personal Vision, Not Someone Else's."

Principles About Obstacles

21) "Setbacks and Failures Are Inevitable, Useful, and Important."
22) "Regret Must Be Tamed, Lest It Eat Alive All Chances for Success."
23) "Our Psyche Is Loath to Move out of Our Comfort Zone."

Principles About Extreme Trials

24) "Desperate Times Demand Desperate Measures."

25) "Bankruptcy Is a Last Resort, Not a Resort."

Appendix 2

Common Hurdles to Accomplishing Financial Success

There are always challenges to undertaking something new. Listed below are some of the more common ones that prevent people from improving their financial lives. See if you can identify with any of them. If you recognize what your personal weaknesses are, then you can better avoid giving in to them.

- Procrastination
- Fear of failure
- Fatigue
- Uncertainty about what you are doing and whether it is the best thing to do
- Lack of self-confidence
- Reluctance to visualize yourself as being successful, perhaps even subconsciously refusing to let yourself be so
- A feeling that you don't *deserve* to be successful— believing that success is for other people who were born with more intelligence, drive, and creativity than you
- The desire for *things* or *experiences* (car, phone, house, computer, clothes, furniture, vacations, entertainment) more than *success*

- Not being able to postpone gratification
- Not being willing to live more frugally now so that you can live *much* better later in life
- Feeling overwhelmed by how much there is to learn and apply
- Laziness—it takes work to educate yourself on financial concepts and principles, and then even more work to actually apply what you learn
- Being uncomfortable about rising up in social stature due to your growing wealth
- Fear that your friends will drop away once you achieve real success
- Not being motivated to try to improve your financial situation
- Not making the deliberate *decision* that you want to change
- Not continuing to learn and apply good financial principles and practices in your life

The Financial Success Sequence

When you assemble a product, it often must be done in a specific sequence of steps. If you attempt to jump ahead and put parts together out of sequence, you may find that it won't go together. You may have to back up and take apart some of what you have already assembled.

Life can be like that. Although there are certainly exceptions, as a general rule, preparatory steps are needed in order to be able to execute other steps. If we understand that, then we can better recognize the need for those preparation steps. Oftentimes, there is no shortcut.

I offer this financial progression sequence for your consideration.

- You can't accumulate wealth without first investing.
- You can't invest without first saving.
- You can't save without first earning.
- You can't earn without first getting an education.
- You can't get an education without first studying.
- You can't study without learning good study habits.

Appendix 4

The Principle
of Bees

Many things about life offer two sides, one good and one bad. Bees are like that. Let's look at this to see if it provides an interesting and useful way to think about the principles of financial success.

Bees offer the rich sweetness of honey, but they also can inflict a painful sting. So the bee has the potential to either offer delight or pain. If you treat bees and a beehive carefully, thoughtfully, with knowledge and restraint, they will offer you the sweet delight of honey.

In the same way, if you learn about and treat the principles of financial success with thoughtfulness and consideration, you will be rewarded with a life of sweet success.

If you treat bees roughly, rudely, and arrogantly, you will pay for it with a sting, or perhaps more than one.

If you are arrogant regarding the principles of financial success, feeling that you can ignore them or trample on them because they won't hurt you, you will find yourself stung by surprise, pain, and disappointment.

If you want to take some honey from a hive, you cannot simply grab it in both hands and shake it vigorously to get out the honeycomb and the honey. The bees will respond with a fury and determination that will shock you. As you run away, swatting at the determined attackers, you realize that you can't get the honey out in that manner.

Just so, you cannot simply grab the principles of financial success and shake out the truth. Alas, you will find that the sweetness of the principles cannot be roughly shaken out any more than the honey can be shaken out of the hive. They must be observed, contemplated, and slowly and thoughtfully lifted out and applied in your life.

Appendix 5

The Stages of Life

Every stage of life is different. Each has its own unique activities, challenges, and decisions to be made. It can be helpful to consciously recognize and consider what stage of life we are in. That enables our expectations to be tempered by an understanding of what is typical for that stage. These stages could be grouped in many different ways, with a variety of characteristics to be included. Here is one suggested list, along with some of the key features of each stage.

Stage 1: Birth to age 18

- Focus on developing **character**, **social skills**, and **study habits**.
- Learn basic social skills, how to learn, and what constitutes good character.

Stage 2: Age 19 to 29

- Focus on **education**.
- Decide what career to pursue.
- Attend college, a trade school, or other forms of education.
- Begin full-time employment in the workforce.

- Experience steep learning curves on a new job or jobs.
- Decide where to live.
- Decide whether to marry and whom to marry.
- Begin having children and have child-rearing costs.
- Focus on *spending* and *buying assets*—furniture, appliances, car, clothing, a house.
- Life insurance is important at this stage, if you have a family.
- Enjoy significant *energy* and *vitality*.

Stage 3: Age 30 to 49

- Focus on *earning*.
- Experience increasingly higher levels of income.
- Advance in your chosen career and continue career-oriented *education*.
- Focus on acquiring more expensive assets.
- Spend significant time and money on child-rearing expenses.
- Children may reach college age by the end of this stage— and college costs begin.
- Life insurance continues to be important at this stage.
- Recognize a little decline in *energy* and *vitality*.

Stage 4: Age 50 to 64

- Focus on *saving*.
- Plateau in your chosen career.

- Income earning years are at their peak.
- Enjoy the empty nest—your children are all financially independent (hopefully!).
- Capitalize on the ability to save a much larger percentage of income.
- Begin to think about retirement.
- Focus on paying off all *debt* before retirement.
- Life insurance becomes less necessary, as children are on their own.
- Observe decreasing physical strength but continued mental and emotional stamina.

Stage 5: Age 65 to 74

- Focus on *investing* and *donating*.
- Begin receiving Social Security as an income supplement.
- Begin Medicare as a form of health insurance.
- Experience the transition into retirement.
- Indulge in lifelong desires—travel, volunteering, grandparenting.
- Focus on managing a lifetime of savings and investments.
- Focus on the importance of maintaining good *health* and *fitness*.
- *Teach* life lessons to your *children* and *grandchildren*.
- *Teach* life lessons to *young people* just starting out in their working years.
- Life insurance is probably no longer needed.
- Focus on finalizing *estate planning*.

Stage 6: Age 75 to 84

- Focus on maintaining good *health* and *fitness*.
- Travel less due to reduced energy levels or declining health.
- Continue to focus on managing your retirement portfolio.
- Emphasize *family* and *friends*.
- Ensure that all estate plans are kept up to date.

Stage 7: Age 85+

- *Treasure* time you get to spend with children, grandchildren, and friends.
- Recognize that your mental acuity is slipping, and be cautious about your investments.
- Continue to ensure that all estate plans are kept up to date.
- Enjoy every additional year you are blessed to get to see and experience!

Appendix 6

The Role of Welfare

Because welfare has become such a prominent part of life in the world today, it's appropriate for us to look at it as we consider all aspects of personal financial management.

If you or your family have never received welfare, then you may elect to skip this discussion. If you're struggling financially, though, it is possible that at some point you may be eligible to receive aid of some type, even if you haven't received it yet. In that case, you may find this to be informative and helpful.

I am not wanting to get political or applaud the way any political party does things. What I *am* trying to do is to help you decide if being on welfare is good for you and your family—first in the short term, then in the long term.

Welfare is an important program in most developed countries in the world. As just one example, in 2019 in the United States, thirty-eight million people used SNAP, the Supplemental Nutrition Assistance Program, also known as food stamps.[20] That's a significant percentage of the US population. Interestingly, whether you think the welfare program in the US is a successful one or not is actually not relevant. What matters is whether welfare is good for *you*, either as an individual or as a family. Is it going to help you achieve long-term financial success? That's what each of us must determine.

Most people are on welfare because they are struggling to survive, for a variety of reasons, and are grateful for the helping hand. They also want to better themselves, get a good job, and work their way off welfare as soon as possible. If you're one of those with that mindset, then I applaud you. Welfare is designed to give you short-term assistance, providing you a way to survive while you get your life back on track. Learning and applying the principles of financial success can hopefully help you in that process.

But some people seem to stay on welfare for an extended period of time, perhaps years. Maybe they would like to better themselves but just can't seem to make it happen. I recognize that every person's situation is different. You may have circumstances in your life that you feel make it impossible for you to rise out of dependence on welfare. Perhaps that is true. I would invite you to read on and consider what I have to say, then weigh whether there might be some things you could do to begin the process of working your way out of welfare.

Why did welfare get started? Because people were starving to death. In the 1930s, for example, during the Dust Bowl days and the Great Depression, there were a shocking number of people starving because they could not get enough to eat. The book *Grapes of Wrath*, by John Steinbeck, is an eloquent story that vividly describes the pain and desperation of that time. Out of compassion for our fellow man, welfare was started to help care for those in dire circumstances. It was a way for every American, through the taxes they pay, to help others.

Short-Term Benefits

The primary benefit of welfare is that it provides a lifeline to those whose life situation is desperate. That may include providing food to those who may not be able to afford food for themselves and their family. It could include providing temporary housing to the homeless. It could include providing clothing to those without means to buy any. And it can include offering counseling and training to enable those struggling to get a job to learn how to provide for themselves and get "back on their feet."

The short-term benefits of the welfare programs are real and certainly helpful to those in need. Many would be unable to survive without them.

Long-Term Benefits and Pitfalls

The long-term benefits are a different matter. While it continues to be a nice source of income, what happens when a person remains on welfare for an extended period of time? There is a trap you can fall into if you aren't careful. Not everyone does, of course, but some do. Let me explain what can occur.

Someone receives food, clothing, and shelter for free, without having to work for it, and begins to think, *This is good. I can get enough to eat without having to do anything, without having to work.* So instead of viewing this assistance with the understanding that they need to work to get back on their feet as soon as possible, they begin to spend their mental energy trying to precisely understand the criteria for receiving welfare. They "work" to become experts at maximizing the amount of welfare they can receive, from as many sources as possible. Once that mindset takes hold, they are no longer trying to work their way *off* welfare, but rather they are seeking to stay *on* it as long as possible. That approach will act as an anchor, effectively keeping them in a perpetual state of poverty.

Is it reasonable to expect someone to try to work for a living, and eventually no longer need welfare? Or is that harsh, considering all of the unfortunate circumstances that can befall someone? Perhaps pity and sympathy are what is needed, you may think.

Let me suggest a hypothetical situation. If your next-door neighbor falls and injures themself so that they can't mow their lawn for a month, you may be willing to help them out by mowing their lawn for them while they're recovering. But once they have recovered and can now mow their own lawn, you assume that they will resume mowing it themselves. What if your neighbor figures out a way to get a doctor friend to write them a note that states they shouldn't mow for another month, but it's apparent that they are fully healed, which they even admit? What if after the additional month goes by, they continue to come up with one excuse after another as to why they can't mow, even though they are fully recovered? It has become apparent that they simply don't want to mow their lawn. They want you to keep doing it. Does that motivate you to want to continue to mow their lawn for them—for weeks, months, or longer? No. You expect them to resume caring for their own lawn themselves.

Yet when people make it their goal to focus on maximizing the welfare they receive, rather than working to get off welfare, that is what they are doing. Money to pay for welfare comes from the government treasury. The government gets their money from every citizen and company in the form of taxes. So every penny that is paid to someone on welfare is paid by you and me, by every taxpayer in the country.

What happens to your mind and your heart after you're dependent on someone else for an extended period of time? This could be in the form of a generous relative who is helping you out each month, or it could be in the form of various government aid programs. You become accustomed to the lifestyle that the extra income affords you to have. It becomes your habit to receive and use that money every month. You eventually come to expect it to be there, as though it is your right. You feel entitled to it. Once that happens, your motivation to better yourself is weakened. Why should you go to night school to learn a trade, or go to community college classes in the evenings to get a degree? You have become content where you are in life. But your contentment is built on the expectation that this outside income will continue perpetually, and that is not guaranteed. You also will never get away from a tiny tingling of guilt because you did not earn that extra money coming in; it was given to you. Donated. You were the recipient of charity.

Gaining Independence

It is a natural human desire to be independent. That's why individual rights and job opportunities are the goal of millions of people in the world. It is an empowering feeling to know that you are completely independent of anyone else. You can financially take care of yourself and your family without assistance.

If you desire to work your way off welfare, how do you do it? The key to climbing out of welfare is getting a good job. How do you do that? First, you must get the education and training needed to qualify you as a good job candidate. Then you must learn job-hunting skills so you can market yourself to prospective employers, and so you can learn about, and effectively pursue, those good jobs that are available.

There are many opportunities available for education. Adult learning centers teach a variety of topics. Local community colleges offer an assortment of job-related classes to help you advance in your skills. Chapter 12, which focuses on earning, explores this point in more detail.

What about language? What if English isn't your first language? Then you will be handicapped in your search for a good job. My recommendation? Take language classes at the local adult education center. America is great at providing opportunities to learn English at no cost. There are literacy council offices all across the country whose primary aim is to increase literacy among their local population. The better you can make your conversational English, the more doors will open to you in terms of jobs. It will also just make your life much easier.

Transition to Earned Income

Another aspect of welfare that you must understand and expect is that the more you earn and the more income you generate on your own, the less welfare you will receive. As your income goes up, your welfare payment goes down. So your net financial situation may not *appear* to be changing. An important dynamic is occurring though. You are steadily shifting the source of your income from welfare to *earned* income. That shifting will continue, with earnings going up and welfare going down, until you no longer qualify to receive any assistance. At that point, the welfare does not go down any further, it simply ends. From that point onward, every additional dollar you earn is no longer offset by a decrease in welfare benefits. You will have the freedom to continue to grow your income through pay raises, job promotions, and career education without any concern for the impact to your welfare benefits.

Welfare Legacy

Guard against letting welfare become a generational habit for you. Some families see their legacy as teaching their children the inner workings of the welfare system so they can shrewdly maximize the amount that *their children* receive. It is almost a game—where they and the government are opponents, trying to outsmart and outmaneuver one another. With that mindset, their goals become how to qualify for as many aid packages as possible, and how to keep themselves eligible instead of learning a new trade or profession so that they no longer need any assistance. If you do that, your dependence on welfare can carry on for generations. Is that the legacy you want to leave, teaching your children to shirk working whenever possible, to "game" the system so that they figure out how to maximize their aid?

A better approach is to teach your children that living independently, free of needing assistance from anyone else, is the appropriate goal for an adult. I encourage you to inspire them to study hard so they can be successful students, which will eventually lead to attaining an education, which then leads to increased job opportunities. Getting a good job is the bottom rung on the ladder they can use to climb out of poverty.

If you are part of a family or social circle that relies heavily on welfare, you will need to push back against that in order to break free from it. You must come to see the value and worth of weaning yourself and your family off welfare before you can be motivated to do so.

Recognize that if you do succeed in getting off welfare and are delighted with the results, you will then influence others in your social circle to begin working to get off welfare as well. You will be admired and respected for your success and be a positive role model to others.

Conclusion

I am on your side. I want you to succeed. My goal is not to berate you and make you feel guilty if you receive welfare. My goal is to help you to grow into a state of being financially independent and, even more than that, successful. I want to help you to be the best you can be. You *can* work your way off welfare. Almost anyone can, with time. But you have to *want* to do that. You have to be willing to work against the strong pull of that unearned check that comes in the mail or gets deposited into your bank account. It actually is like a form of addiction, so you have to approach it like you're breaking an addictive habit.

As one final point, remember that all the principles outlined in this book still apply, whether you are receiving welfare or not. So the more you learn, understand, and apply them, the quicker you can grow your income, manage your finances well, and work your way off welfare.

My hope is that you will be inspired and motivated to keep trying and working to get to the point where your earned income completely supports you, and you no longer need to receive any assistance. That is the path that will give you the greatest amount of personal satisfaction and pride in what you have accomplished.

Appendix 7

The COVID-19 Pandemic

2020, 2021, and now 2022 have been forever marked by the COVID-19 pandemic. All aspects of life were affected, including people's financial lives. In spite of the extraordinary nature of this event, though, the principles of financial success still held true. We still had to decide how to earn, spend, borrow, save, invest, and donate our money. Actions still had consequences. Trust was still important. All of these principles, just like the law of gravity, still acted in the same way.

What was perhaps different was the dominant importance of adaptability. Life changed so drastically, and in so many ways, that our ability to make changes—and still more changes—in order to survive and thrive was sorely tested. In the end, I believe that history will show that humankind was up to the task.

Appendix 8

Bitcoin and Cryptocurrency

Cryptocurrency has grown in importance over the past few years until now it is a dominant investment topic in the world of finance. Some believe it will eventually become the new reserve currency in the world, unseating the US dollar from that long-held position. The prospect has, in fact, been dangled that it may become the de facto global currency as well, one which would effectively replace the currency of every country in the world.

Others view cryptocurrency as a fad that will eventually fade in importance. They feel that it may remain in use for years but will not ever become a currency. It will simply be an investment, which may go up or down in value in the marketplace where it is traded, just as stocks and many other types of investment.

I have chosen to not include any other discussion of this topic in the book other than this brief appendix, because it's unclear the role that it will eventually play in world markets and economies. It is certainly an interesting phenomenon, though, and one which bears watching.

Notes

1. Joe Resendiz, "Average Credit Card Debt in America: 2021," ValuePenquin, accessed August 2, 2021. https://www. valuepenguin.com/average-credit-card-debt.

2. "Student Loan Debt, A Current Picture of Student Loan Borrowing and Repayment in the United States," Nitro College, November 30, 2022. https://www.nitrocollege.com/research/ average-student-loan-debt.

3. "Student Loan Debt," Nitro College.

4. "Report on the Economic Well-Being of U.S. Households in 2018–May 2019," Board of Governors of the Federal Reserve System, May 28, 2019. https://www.federalreserve.gov/ publications/2019-economic-well-being-of-us-households- in-2018-dealing-with-unexpected-expenses.htm.

5. Hillary Hoffower, "60% of Millennials Earning over $100,000 Say They're Living Paycheck to Paycheck," Business Insider, September 16, 2021. https://www.businessinsider.com/high- earning-henry-millennials-six-figure-salaries-feel-broke- 2021-6.

6. "Definition of Money," Merriam-Webster, accessed August 8, 2021. https://www.merriam-webster.com/dictionary/money.

7. "Student Loan Debt," Nitro College.

8. Bill Fay, "Key Figures Behind America's Consumer Debt," Debt. org, May 13, 2021. https://www.debt.org/faqs/americans-in-debt/.

9. Matt Frankel and Kamran Rosen, "Credit Card Debt Statistics for 2020," The Ascent, July 16, 2020. https://www.fool.com/the-ascent/research/credit-card-debt-statistics/.

10. Cambridge Dictionary, accessed August 3, 2021. https://dictionary.cambridge.org/us/dictionary/english/borrow.

11. Cambridge Dictionary.

12. "Tuition Costs of Colleges and Universities," National Center for Education Statistics, 2021. https://nces.ed.gov/fastfacts/display.asp?id=76.

13. Frankel and Rosen, "Credit Card Debt."

14. Davide Scigliuzzo, "Charging 589% Interest in the Pandemic Is a Booming Business," Bloomberg, May 17, 2021. https://www.bloomberg.com/graphics/2021-payday-loan-lenders-apple-news/.

15. Kendra Cherry, "What Is Altruism?" Verywellmind, April 14, 2021. https://www.verywellmind.com/what-is-altruism-2794828.

16. Monica Vaca, "The Top Frauds of 2020," Federal Trade Commission, February 4, 2021. https://www.consumer.ftc.gov/blog/2021/02/top-frauds-2020.

17. Vaca, "The Top Frauds."

18. Emma Fletcher, "Scams starting on social media proliferate in early 2020," Federal Trade Commission, October 21, 2020. https://www.ftc.gov/news-events/data-visualizations/data-spotlight/2020/10/scams-starting-social-media-proliferate-early-2020.

19. Goodreads, accessed August 3, 2021. https://www.goodreads.com/quotes/787509-no-one-can-make-you-feel-inferior-without-your-permission.

20. Christianna Silva, "Food Insecurity in The U.S. By The Numbers," npr.org, September 27, 2020. https://www.npr.org/2020/09/27/912486921/food-insecurity-in-the-u-s-by-the-numbers.

Tables

Bibliography

"American Eagle Silver Bullion Coins." United States Mint, 2019. https://www.usmint.gov/coins/coin-medal-programs/american-eagle/silver-bullion.

Cambridge Dictionary, accessed August 3, 2021. https://dictionary.cambridge.org/us/dictionary/english/borrow.

"Canceling a contract within three days." Nolo.com, accessed September 27, 2021. https://www.nolo.com/legal-encyclopedia/canceling-contract-within-three-days-30246.html.

Cherry, Kendra. "What is Altruism?" Verywellmind, April 14, 2021. https://www.verywellmind.com/what-is-altruism-2794828.

"Definition of Money," Merriam-Webster, accessed August 8, 2021. https://www.merriam-webster.com/dictionary/money.

Fay, Bill. "Key Figures Behind America's Consumer Debt," Debt.org, May 13, 2021. https://www.debt.org/faqs/americans-in-debt/.

Fletcher, Emma. "Scams starting on social media proliferate in early 2020," Federal Trade Commission, October 21, 2020. https://www.ftc.gov/news-events/data-visualizations/data-spotlight/2020/10/scams-starting-social-media-proliferate-early-2020.

Frankel, Matt and Rosen, Kamran. "Credit Card Debt Statistics for 2020," The Ascent, July 16, 2020. https://www.fool.com/the-ascent/research/credit-card-debt-statistics/.

Goodreads, accessed August 3, 2021. https://www.goodreads.com/quotes/787509-no-one-can-make-you-feel-inferior-without-your-permission.

Hoffower, Hillary. "60% of Millennials Earning over $100,000 Say They're Living Paycheck to Paycheck," Business Insider, September 16, 2021. https://www.businessinsider.com/high-earning-henry-millennials-six-figure-salaries-feel-broke-2021-6.

"Report on the Economic Well-Being of U.S. Households in 2018" - May 2019, Board of Governors of the Federal Reserve System, May 28, 2019. https://www.federalreserve.gov/publications/2019-economic-well-being-of-us-households-in-2018-dealing-with-unexpected-expenses.htm.

Resendiz, Joe. "Average Credit Card Debt in America: 2021," ValuePenquin, accessed August 2, 2021. https://www.valuepenguin.com/average-credit-card-debt.

Scigliuzzo, Davide. "Charging 589% Interest in the Pandemic Is a Booming Business", Bloomberg, May 17, 2021. https://www.bloomberg.com/graphics/2021-payday-loan-lenders/.

Silva, Christianna. "Food Insecurity In The U.S. By The Numbers," npr.org, September 27, 2020. https://www.npr.org/2020/09/27/912486921/food-insecurity-in-the-u-s-by-the-numbers.

"Student Loan Debt, A Current Picture of Student Loan Borrowing and Repayment in the United States," Nitro College, November 30, 2022. https://www.nitrocollege.com/research/average-student-loan-debt.

"Tuition Costs of Colleges and Universities," National Center for Education Statistics, 2021. https://nces.ed.gov/fastfacts/display.asp?id=76.

Vaca, Monica. "The Top Frauds of 2020, Federal Trade Commission," February 4, 2021. https://www.consumer.ftc.gov/blog/2021/02/top-frauds-2020.

"Winner in the Battle of the Brews: Dunkin' Donuts Beat Starbucks in Independent Nationwide Taste Test," Dunkindonuts, October 20, 2008. https://news.dunkindonuts.com/news/winner-in-the-battle-of-the-brews:-dunkin-donuts-beat-starbucks-in-independent-nationwide-taste-test.

Further Reading

Bolles, Richard Nelson. *What Color Is Your Parachute?* Berkeley: Ten Speed Press, 1970.

Canfield, Jack. *The Success Principles*. New York: HarperCollins, 2005.

CESI Services. Consumer Education Services, Inc. Accessed August 4, 2021. https://www.cesisolutions.org/services-2/. (CESI: a non-profit committed to empowering and inspiring consumers nationwide to make wise financial decisions and live debt-free.)

Danko, William D. and Stanley, Thomas J. *The Millionaire Next Door*. New York: Pocket Books, 1996.

DeNicola, Louis. *How Does Compound Interest Work?* Experian. September 16, 2019. https://www.experian.com/blogs/ask-experian/how-compound-interest-works/.

Dimnet, Ernest. *The Art of Thinking*. New York: Simon & Schuster, 1928. (This is the original edition. It has been reprinted multiple times by various publishers.)

Doyle, Alison. *Free Career Aptitude and Career Assessment Tests.* The Balance Careers. May 19, 2021. https://www.thebalancecareers. com/free-career-aptitude-tests-2059813.

Find the Job That Fits Your Life. Glassdoor. Accessed August 4, 2021. https://www.glassdoor.com/job/index.htm (To get employees' ratings of companies.)

Hartill, Robin. *This Is Why FIRE Is a Wildly Unrealistic Retirement Strategy for Most People.* The Motley Fool. October 21, 2020. https://www.fool.com/investing/2020/10/21/this-is-why-fire-is-a-wildly-unrealistic-retiremen/.

Kiyosaki, Robert T. *Rich Dad Poor Dad.* Scottsdale: Plata Publishing, 2011.

Laja, Peep. *Purchase Decisions: 9 Things to Know About Influencing Customers.* CXL. March 15, 2021. https://cxl.com/blog/9-things-to-know-about-influencing-purchasing-decisions/. (Interesting article on why people choose to buy something.)

MacDonald, Jay and Steele, Jason. *The History of Credit Cards,* CreditCards.com, May 24, 2021. https://www.creditcards.com/credit-card-news/history-of-credit-cards/. (Credit cards have become such an integral part of contemporary society that it is hard to believe this hasn't always been the case. In the history of the world, though, they are a very recent development.)

Murray, Peter Noel. *How Emotions Influence What We Buy*. Psychology Today. February 26, 2013. https://www.psychologytoday.com/us/blog/inside-the-consumer-mind/201302/how-emotions-influence-what-we-buy.

Rakoczy, Christy. *Best Budgeting Software*. Investopedia. April 14, 2021. https://www.investopedia.com/personal-finance/best-budgeting-software/.

Ramsey, Dave. *Financial Peace Revisited*. New York: Viking Penguin, 2003.

The Strong Interest Inventory® Test. Career Assessment Site. Accessed November 25, 2021. https://careerassessmentsite.com/tests/strong-tests/about-the-strong-interest-inventory/.

About the Author

Randy Todhunter has had the opportunity to explore a variety of disciplines. He studied English literature at Washington University in St. Louis and ministry at Manhattan Christian College in Manhattan, Kansas. His final undergraduate work was at Kansas State University, where he graduated with a BA in Computer Science and was inducted into the Phi Beta Kappa Academic Honor Society. Randy later earned an MBA from the University of Arkansas.

He served as an electrician in the US Coast Guard for four years and learned a lot about himself during that enlistment.

For most of his career, he worked in IT management for a Fortune 1000 logistics and transportation company in Arkansas. In addition to facilitating software development, he also served a stint there as the manager of recruiting and training. He was selected by his employer to be the Partners in Education corporate representative to two local high schools and an elementary school. He enjoyed setting up a pen pal program and later a mentoring program as part of that responsibility, which gave volunteer employees an opportunity to interact with and help individual students. He was honored to receive the citywide Partner of the Year award shortly before retiring.

Randy enjoys managing his personal investment portfolio and helping others learn how to invest, particularly in the stock market.

He has had the opportunity to co-lead classes of Dave Ramsey's Financial Peace University at his local church and has taught business classes as an adjunct instructor in the Fort Smith offsite program of John Brown University. He has also served as a volunteer AARP Tax-Aide Counselor, assisting others with preparing their annual taxes. He was inspired, in part, to write this book after he observed taxpayers who were earnestly seeking additional financial coaching.

He enjoys nature and hiking in the wooded hills of the Ozark and Ouachita Mountains and snow skiing in Colorado. For many years he was an avid motorcyclist but has retired from that and now owns a Corvette for when he wants a weekend outing. He makes his home in Arkansas with his wife and their pet parrot, Cheeky.

Perhaps most importantly, Randy enjoys writing and hopes to help others through his words.